PORTRAIT MINIATURES FROM SCOTTISH PRIVATE COLLECTIONS

SUPPORTED BY DUNARD FUND

PORTRAIT MINIATURES FROM SCOTTISH PRIVATE COLLECTIONS

STEPHEN LLOYD

NATIONAL GALLERIES OF SCOTLAND

MMVI

Published by the Trustees of the
National Galleries of Scotland for the exhibition
Portrait Miniatures from Scottish Private Collections
held at the Scottish National Portrait Gallery, Edinburgh
from 14 July to 29 October 2006

ISBN 1 903278 79 1 (978 1 903278 79 6)

Photography by Antonia Reeve, A.C. Cooper Ltd and Richard Wellsby
Designed and typeset in Adobe Minion MM by Dalrymple
Printed in Belgium by Die Keure

Front jacket: Samuel Cooper
Lady Amelia Ann Sophia Stanley, Marchioness of Atholl
[18]

Back jacket: John Linnell
General William Moore
[91]

LENDERS

Blair Charitable Trust
The Duke of Buccleuch and Queensberry KT
The Earl of Elgin and Kincardine KT
The Duke of Hamilton and Brandon
The Earl of Home CVO CBE
Major Malcolm R.S. Macrae
John Murray
Traquair House Charitable Trust
The Earl of Wemyss and March KT
and others who prefer to remain anonymous

FOREWORD

Over the course of the last decade the Scottish National Portrait Gallery has made strenuous efforts not only to raise the profile of the portrait miniature within Scotland, but also to bring these exquisite works of art to the attention of both our regular visitors and new audiences. To this end the Portrait Gallery has mounted an annual series of exhibitions supported by scholarly catalogues. The Gallery has also sought to acquire suitable works for the collection whenever they have come onto the market and when funds have permitted. Highlights from the national collection were exhibited at the Portrait Gallery in 2004 as *Portrait Miniatures from the National Galleries of Scotland.* Last year the Gallery displayed *Portrait Miniatures from the Merchiston Collection*, a fine group of seventy-six works that has been promised as a future bequest to the Portrait Gallery.

Our dedication to the portrait miniature has encouraged a number of private collectors to place their collections on long-term loan to the Portrait Gallery. In 2001 an exhibition was mounted and a catalogue was produced showcasing *Portrait Miniatures from the Clarke Collection*, featuring outstanding works by British and continental artists from the late sixteenth to the early nineteenth century. The second exhibition, *Portrait Miniatures from the Dumas Egerton Collection*, was held in 2002, with a selection from over 700 signed works by artists working in Britain over a similar time frame. This was followed by an exhibition of *Portrait Miniatures from the Daphne Foskett Collection*, featuring a selection of works by British artists from the mid-seventeenth to the mid-nineteenth century. Alongside this loan to the Portrait Gallery from the family of the late Daphne Foskett, the post-war doyenne of the study of the portrait miniature, has been the deposit in 1999 of her working papers and photographic collection. This archive has already been of great use to scholars and students working in the field.

This current exhibition and catalogue, *Portrait Miniatures from Scottish Private Collections*, presents to the public a selection of British, French and Swiss miniatures dating from the early seventeenth to the mid-nineteenth century. These works, which have been selected for their aesthetic quality and historical interest, have been borrowed from private collections across Scotland. Miniatures not previously seen in Edinburgh have been generously loaned from the renowned collection belonging to the Duke of Buccleuch and Queensberry. Other more famous works from that collection were lent to the Portrait Gallery in 1996–7 and 2004. This catalogue takes forward the research published by the National Galleries in *Portrait Miniatures from the Collection of the Duke of Buccleuch* in 1996. We are most grateful to all the lenders to this exhibition, without whose generosity this show – the first of its kind – would have been impossible to mount. Many of the lenders have also kindly provided invaluable information for this catalogue. As with all the other exhibitions and catalogues in the series, this project has been researched and organised by Dr Stephen Lloyd, senior curator at the Portrait Gallery. He would like to thank all the owners of the miniatures for their assistance and advice, as well as James Berry, Emma and John Dodd, Graeme Gollan, David Lavender, Sue Makin, Antonia Reeve, Alice Thompson and William Zachs for their support in various aspects of this exhibition and catalogue. Finally, special thanks must be given to Dunard Fund, which is not only generously supporting this exhibition and publication, but has also had the foresight to support the whole six-year programme of exhibitions and catalogues devoted to portrait miniatures at the Scottish National Portrait Gallery.

JOHN LEIGHTON
Director-General, National Galleries of Scotland

JAMES HOLLOWAY
Director, Scottish National Portrait Gallery

PORTRAIT MINIATURES FROM SCOTTISH PRIVATE COLLECTIONS

The portrait miniature, painted in watercolour on vellum or ivory, was a highly specific form of intimate image-making that was practised by artists across Europe. The miniature's origins are found in early sixteenth-century Renaissance manuscript illumination and its demise was heralded by the invention of photography in the mid-nineteenth century. Initially the portrait miniature acted as a portable gift in diplomatic marriage negotiations at the royal courts of northern Europe. However, it was among the social elite of post-Reformation Elizabethan and Jacobean England that the creation and exchange of miniatures, or limnings, took hold most securely, as epitomised by the dazzling portraiture of Nicholas Hilliard and Isaac Oliver [1]. Their limnings were often set inside jewelled lockets that were worn on the body as a token of love or loyalty. These courtly and emotional functions, which were integral to the whole process of commissioning, giving and wearing miniatures, continued throughout the history of the format.

During the late seventeenth and early eighteenth centuries, the continental tradition of painting portrait miniatures was closely allied to court culture. However, in Britain during this period miniaturists were increasingly prospering outside the court, especially among the wealthier sectors of society such as the landed gentry and the merchant classes. During the late eighteenth century portrait miniatures became increasingly popular across the major population centres of Britain and Ireland, and throughout Europe. Miniatures continued to function principally as portable likenesses of loved ones, especially in their absence. They acted not only as objects of affection, such as engagement or marriage portraits, but also as focal points of memory, and in particular as memorials to the recently deceased. During the final phase of the miniature, just around the advent of less expensive photography during the 1840s, artists increased the size of the painted ivory surface in an attempt to compete with small oil paintings as well as with portrait drawings and watercolours on paper. These larger 'cabinet' miniatures were mainly intended for domestic display within room settings.

The miniatures in this exhibition have been selected both for their intrinsic quality and for their historical significance. An attempt has also been made to show a representative selection of works across two and a half centuries, from the early seventeenth to the mid-nineteenth century. The earliest miniature in the exhibition is by the Jacobean limner Isaac Oliver, which depicts the famous poet and divine *John Donne* [1]. From the Caroline period is a portrait of the Persian diplomat *Sir Robert Shirley* [3] by Peter Oliver. Also painted during Charles I's reign are three fascinating limnings by John Hoskins: his *Self-portrait* [2], as well as *Mary Villiers, Lady Herbert, later Duchess of Lennox and Richmond* [5] and *James Hamilton, 3rd Marquess and 1st Duke of Hamilton* [4]. The latter is also shown in two later portraits, one in oils after Van Dyck [6] and another miniature made towards the end of his life by David Des Granges [9]. Charles I is also included in a tiny portrait that was incorporated into a memorial ring after his execution in 1649 [10]. The work of Hoskins's nephew and outstanding pupil, Samuel Cooper, is well represented with five miniatures, including *Sir Charles Compton* [7] from the Civil War period; *William Douglas, Earl of Selkirk, later 3rd Duke of Hamilton* [12] from the Interregnum; and the beautifully preserved *Lady Amelia Ann Sophia Stanley, Marchioness of Atholl* [18] from after the Restoration, which is signed and dated 1667.

There are a number of important miniatures representing the Jacobites, notably *Prince James Francis Edward Stuart* [30] by Jacqueline de La Boissière; *Prince Charles Edward Stuart* [43] by John Daniel Kamm after Maurice-Quentin de La Tour; and *Prince Henry Benedict Stuart* [38] by Jean-Etienne Liotard. Three key members of one of the leading exiled Jacobite families, that of the Dukes of Perth, are also included in this selection, with *James Drummond, 4th Earl and 1st titular Duke of Perth* [27] painted by Peter Cross in the 1680s; *James Drummond, 5th Earl and 2nd titular Duke of Perth* portrayed by C. Tassis after François de Troy [28] in 1694 and later by Benjamin Arlaud [31]; and *James Drummond, 6th Earl and 3rd titular Duke of Perth* [41] painted in enamel on copper by Jean-André Rouquet.

Significant portrait miniatures painted in Britain during the first half of the eighteenth century include two works by Bernard Lens III, who was the first artist to make a career painting on ivory. These are *General Hatton Compton* [37] and the full-length cabinet miniature after Sir Godfrey Kneller of *James Douglas, Earl of Arran, later 4th Duke of Hamilton* [32], which was probably painted after his death in a duel in 1712. Miniatures painted in enamels were also particularly fashionable at this date, as seen in examples by Christian Friedrich Zincke [35, 40], Gervase Spencer [44] and William Prewett [36]. Of outstanding interest from this period is the diplomatic gift, comprising a gold locket, dating around 1744–5, which incorporates miniatures on vellum by Jean-Etienne Liotard [42] of *Maria Teresa, Empress of Austria*, her sister the *Duchess Maria Anna*, together with an enamel of *Anne Murray Keith*, who was daughter of Robert Keith, the British ambassador in Vienna. Another rare work on vellum attributed to Liotard is included in this exhibition, which can be dated to the second half of the 1760s, showing *Francis, Charteris of Amisfield, later 7th Earl of Wemyss* [51] on his Grand Tour while passing through Geneva.

The second half of the eighteenth century witnessed a huge growth in the numbers of miniaturists working across the British Isles and Europe. The selection here includes many of the more prominent artists working in London at that date, including Samuel Cotes [49], George Engleheart [54, 70], Philip Jean [66, 69], Andrew Plimer [63, 64] Samuel Shelley [68] and seven examples by the most famous miniaturist of the period, Richard Cosway. Among the Scottish artists who were working in Edinburgh, focus is placed on Sir Henry Raeburn – much better known for his oil portraits – with four miniatures from the 1770s, including *Andrew Wood* [57], as well as the pair of *James Gilliland* [55] and his wife *Elizabeth MacMurray* [56]. Four miniatures are also included by Archibald Skirving, a pastellist of exceptional quality who worked mainly in Edinburgh. Dating from the late 1790s, this group features *Charles-Philippe, Comte d'Artois, later Charles* X [71], as well as *James Drummond, Baron Perth and Lord Drummond of Stobhall* [72] and his daughter *Clementina Sarah Drummond, later Baroness Willoughby de Eresby* [73].

The miniatures selected for this exhibition have been drawn principally from Scottish family collections such as those commissioned by the Dukes of Hamilton and the Earls of Wemyss, as well as from the well-known ancestral seats of Traquair

House and Blair Castle, which are open to the public. Other miniatures have been acquired more recently, sometimes being added into existing family collections of portraits [43, 69, 84]. However, undoubtedly the greatest collection of miniatures ever formed by a Scottish collector was the assemblage of more than 750 works acquired in London during the middle and late nineteenth century by Walter Francis Montagu-Douglas-Scott, 5th Duke of Buccleuch and 7th Duke of Queensberry (1806–1884).[1]

This magnate was one of the great Victorian philanthropists, who did much to maintain and improve the extensive Buccleuch estates in Scotland, in particular around Bowhill in the Borders and the Queensberry estate around Drumlanrig in Dumfriesshire. However, much of his life was spent at Dalkeith House near Edinburgh, where he was the host during the visits of George IV in 1822 and Queen Victoria in 1842. The 5th Duke also lived at Montagu House in Whitehall, London, where he displayed the miniatures.

Walter Francis was also an important industrial developer. Between 1835 and 1842 he built Granton harbour in Edinburgh at his own expense, reputedly at a cost of over half a million pounds. He also played a significant role in the development of Barrow-in-Furness. A staunch conservative, he was made Lord Privy Seal in Peel's administration in 1842, a post which he held for four years, when he was briefly appointed Lord President of Council. Later in life the 5th Duke enjoyed widespread influence in Scotland. By the time of his death the Buccleuch estates were not only the second largest to be retained in private hands in Britain, but they were also producing the second highest gross income.

The 5th Duke's distinguished public life and career were reflected in the many honours he received. He was created a Knight of the Thistle in 1830 and a Knight of the Garter in 1835. In 1831 he was appointed President of the Highland Agricultural Society; in 1862 he was elected to the Presidency of the Society of Antiquaries, and, in 1867, to a similar position in the British Association. He also received a number of honours from British universities, including a DCL from Oxford in 1834 and LLDs from Cambridge and Edinburgh in 1842 and 1874 respectively, while in 1877 he was elected Chancellor of Glasgow University. In addition, he held the offices of High Steward of Westminster, and Lord Lieutenant and Sheriff of Midlothian and Roxburgh.[2]

As well as the miniature painted by

Christina Robertson in 1832 [fig.1], the 5th Duke was portrayed many times in oils – by William Ingalton (in 1822), Sir Francis Grant, H.W. Pickersgill, Sir Daniel Macnee (1877), and C. Knighton Warren (1884), and also in a painting and chalk drawing (1864) by George Richmond. However, the most public monument to him was the posthumous bronze statue made by J. Edgar Boehm in 1887–8, which was erected on an ornate pedestal – designed by Sir Robert Rowand Anderson – opposite the west door of the High Kirk of St Giles, in Edinburgh's Parliament Square.

Walter Francis had succeeded to his titles in 1819 at the age of thirteen, on the death of his father, Charles, 4th Duke of Buccleuch and 6th Duke of Queensberry. It appears that the 5th Duke had already inherited about 150 miniatures from his grandmother, Elizabeth Montagu, Duchess of Buccleuch (1743–1827), the wife of Henry, 3rd Duke of Buccleuch (1746–1812). From the latter, the 5th Duke certainly inherited Scott family miniatures including portraits of their ancestor James Scott, Duke of Monmouth and Buccleuch (1649–1685), the natural son of Charles II and Lucy Walter. However, it is uncertain if the Montagu collection of miniatures was originally formed by Elizabeth Montagu, or whether she had inherited it from her mother Mary, Duchess of Montagu (1712–1775). It was certainly Mary Montagu, together with her husband George Brudenell, 4th Earl of Cardigan, later Duke of Montagu (1712–1790), who acquired many of the finest old master pictures for Montagu House in London. Today the collection is now dispersed between the three main Buccleuch homes of Bowhill in the Scottish Borders, Drumlanrig Castle in Dumfriesshire, and Boughton House in Northamptonshire.

Walter Francis's early childhood was marked by a close friendship with Sir Walter Scott, who guided the young duke, notably while he was acting as host at Dalkeith House to George IV during his visit to Scotland in 1822. Perhaps it was the impact of this event, combined with the influence of the great historical novelist – whose famous Romantic portrait by Raeburn was acquired by the 5th Duke in 1826 – that inspired Walter Francis to collect portrait miniatures so assiduously.[3] An early indication of the 5th Duke's interest in miniatures was in 1831–2 when, as a young man, he commissioned Christina Robertson's magnificent pair of cabinet portraits of himself and his wife, Lady Charlotte Anne Thynne, youngest daughter of Thomas, 2nd Marquess of Bath.[4]

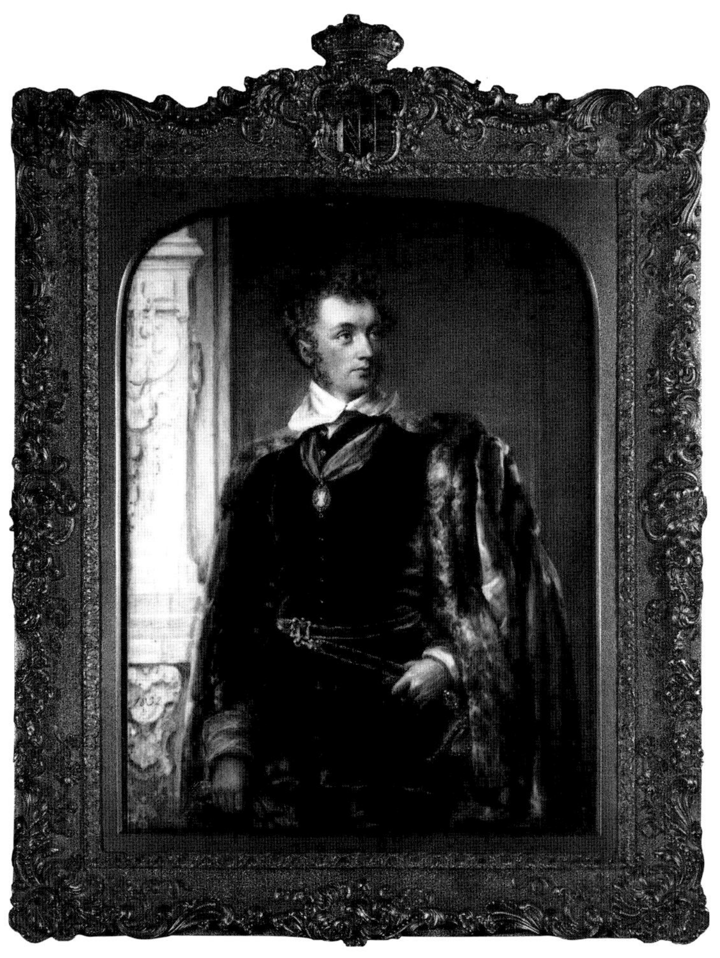

Fig.1 *Walter Francis, 5th Duke of Buccleuch and 7th Duke of Queensberry (1806–1884)*, by Christina Robertson, watercolour on ivory, 1832. In the collection of the Duke of Buccleuch & Queensberry KT

The 5th Duke is first known to have acquired historical miniatures in 1842 at the famous sale of the collection of the great antiquarian *Horatio (or Horace) Walpole, 4th Earl of Orford (1717–1797)* [36], held at his celebrated neo-Gothic villa of Strawberry Hill in Twickenham, to the south-west of London. Walpole had assembled the eighteenth century's most important collection of miniatures. Among the portraits bought by Walter Francis at the sale were the following: a Holbein of Catherine Howard, the fifth wife of Henry VIII, which had been in the famous collection of the Earl of Arundel; the small oil on panel of Mary of Guise, mother of Mary Queen of Scots, attributed to Corneille de Lyon; and the Samuel Cooper miniature of an unknown lady, formerly called Lady Heydon. Just over twenty years later the 5th Duke was to acquire another important miniature that had belonged to Walpole and had formerly been in the Strawberry Hill sale, that of Anne Boleyn, the second wife of Henry VIII, painted by Lucas Horenbout, but then considered to be a portrait of Catherine of Aragon by Holbein.

It appears that the 5th Duke acquired the bulk of his collection of miniatures during the twenty-five year period following the Strawberry Hill sale. He was active when significant works became available at the auctions of important collections, such as those of Lord Northwick in 1859, of Matthew Uzielli in 1861, and at the Hamilton Palace sale in 1882. From the Northwick collection Walter Francis acquired the beautiful large portrait drawing by Isaac Oliver of an *Unknown Boy, formerly called Henry, Prince of Wales*, which had been at Strawberry Hill, and the miniature by Samuel Cooper of *Mary Fairfax, Duchess of Buckingham*. At the Uzielli sale the 5th Duke purchased further Coopers, including an unknown gentleman, formerly called *John, 1st Baron Belasyse* and that of *James Scott, Duke of Monmouth and Buccleuch*. At the Hamilton Palace sale Walter Francis purchased the Hoskins head-and-shoulders copy of Van Dyck's full-length oil of *Lady Frances Cranfield, Countess of Dorset* [fig.2]. This cabinet miniature had previously been in both the Northwick collection and at Strawberry Hill, and is still contained within the fine ebony casket, set with silver decorations and Wedgwood medallions with classical figures, that was designed for it by Horace Walpole.

However, the 5th Duke mainly bought his miniatures on the London art market, through the noted print sellers and art dealers Paul and Dominic Colnaghi, who were based in Pall Mall, London. It was through them that he acquired the Horenbouts of Henry VIII and also of Edward VI when he was Prince of Wales. Around 1860 Colnaghi's supplied the duke with two of the most important groups of miniatures for his collection. The first was the frame of eight miniatures by various artists representing the Tudor dynasty. This group had originally been assembled by the great seventeenth-century collector of miniatures, Charles I. In 1862 the duke acquired his most famous group of miniatures through Colnaghi's for £325: the three portraits by Cooper of the Cromwell family, including the celebrated unfinished portrait of the Lord Protector, which had been preserved by his descendants.

From the Colnaghi bills, dating from the 1840s to the 1890s and preserved among the Buccleuch family papers at Bowhill, it is apparent that not only did the art firm supply the 5th and 6th Dukes with miniatures, but also their great collection of old master and portrait prints. In both these areas Walter Francis was a voracious collector. An example of Colnaghi's purchase of miniatures for the duke is a bill submitted on 5 November 1858, relating to three acquisitions:

A Miniature on Vellum of the Old Chevalier [Prince James Francis Edward Stuart] £10–10 —
A d[itt]o. of Philip V of Spain in an old Ormolu Frame £10–10 —
Elizabeth of Bohemia painted in oil by Oliver in an Ivory Case £31–10 —

Colnaghi's also undertook many other aspects of the care of the burgeoning collection of miniatures, including conservation, as can be seen from bills such as these:

3 November 1858: Repairing a Miniature of the Holy Family – 14s —
10 August 1864: Retouching a Miniature in Oil of Katherine of Braganza £1–1 —

Also of interest are the records of Colnaghi's work on the resetting, re-framing and labelling of the miniatures:

1 December 1858: Ormolu Frames & Writing names to 8 miniatures £6–13 —
4 December 1858: A Carved Frame to Hans Oliver: full length Portrait of Clifford, Earl of £2–2 —
28 November 1863: Framing of 25 miniatures in Gilt Bell Metal frames – Putting Gilt scrolls for frames & to 17 Glasses & Retouching £29–15 —
22 August 1864: Cash paid Messrs Chubb & Son for opening Miniature Case – Repairing Lock – New Bolt &c. – 17s —
5 October 1864: Making Gilt [——] Frames & alterations to 50 Miniatures £24–15 —

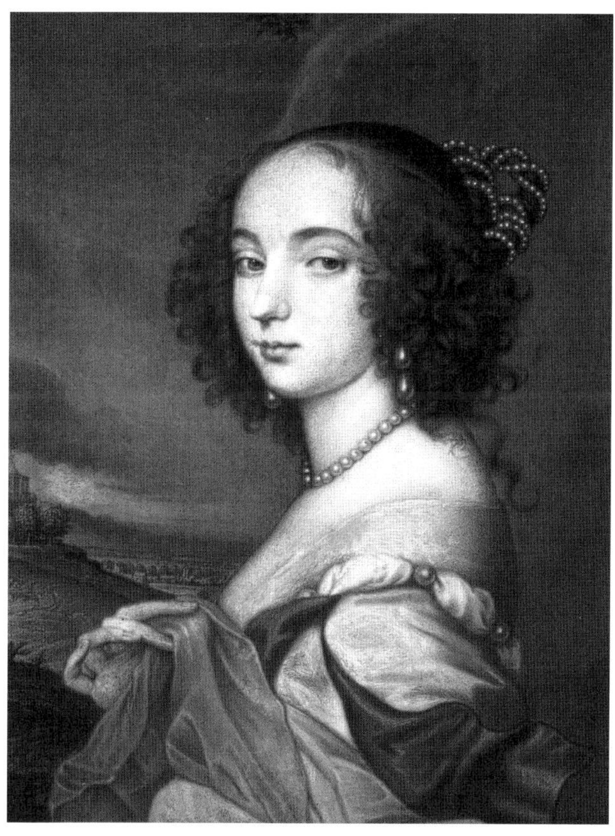

Fig.2 *Lady Frances Cranfield, Countess of Dorset (c.1623–1687)*, by John Hoskins after Sir Anthony van Dyck, bodycolour on vellum, *c.*1637. In the collection of the Duke of Buccleuch & Queensberry KT

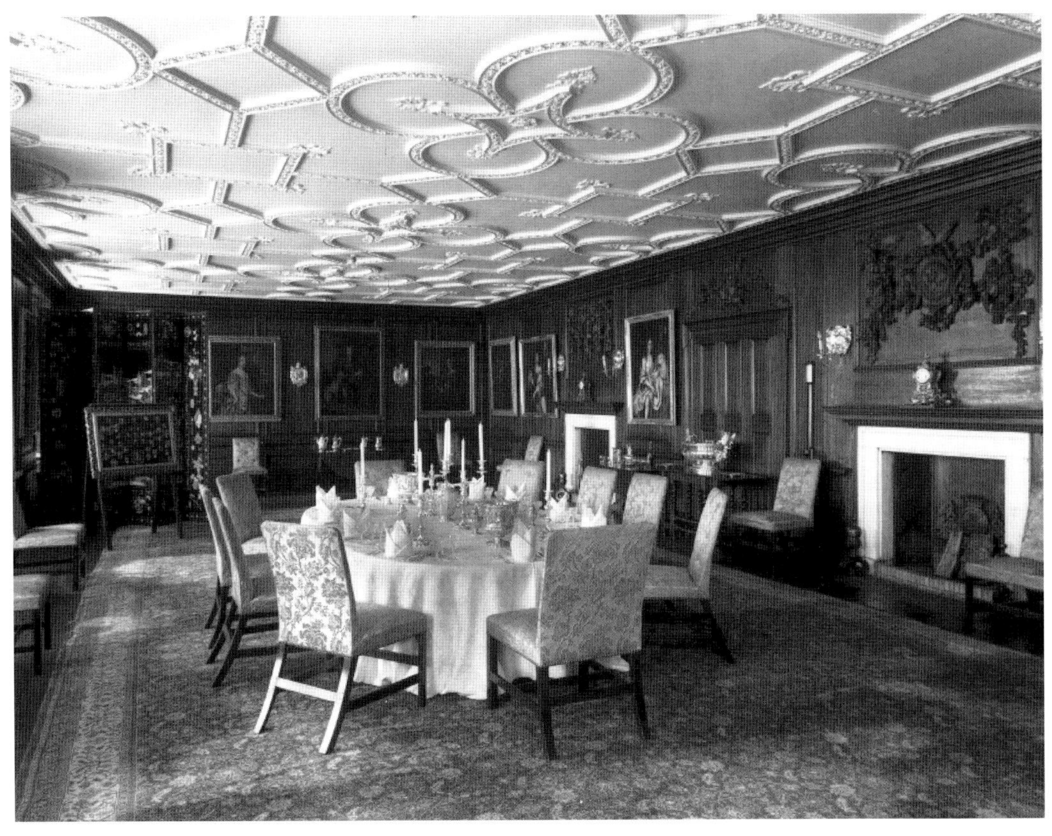

Fig.3 *The Dining Room, Drumlanrig Castle, Dumfriesshire*
A Victorian frame holding forty-two miniatures can be seen on an easel at the end of the room (photograph taken in 1960; courtesy of A. Starkey / *Country Life* photographic library).

24 June 1865: 2 Miniature frames set with Carbuncles £8 — —

The 5th Duke also commissioned the making of a set of more than thirty ornate frames for the miniatures, in each of which up to forty of the portraits could be displayed together:

28 July 1865: 2 Richly carved Gilt Florentine Frames Scroll Oak & Gilt inside to open with Lock & Key £25–15 —
17 December 1870: 3 Richly Craved Scroll pattern Gilt frames with back boards covered with silk velvet to contain miniatures £46–14 —

These ornately carved and gilt wooden frames had backboards covered in red velvet, while red silk covers were also commissioned to protect the miniatures from the destructive effects of sunlight [fig.3]. Most of these frames and some of the covers have survived to this day, and they are still used to store many of the miniatures. In the nineteenth century the miniatures were presented in thirty-four frames at Montagu House in Whitehall, London. The largest group of about twenty frames was displayed in the gallery, with ten frames hung in the duchess's sitting room. In the last room the three miniatures of the Cromwell family were displayed separately in a rosewood box, together with the cabinet miniature by Hoskins after Van Dyck's *Lady Frances Cranfield, Countess of Dorset* [fig.2], which was then thought to be by Peter Oliver and considered to depict Venetia Stanley, Lady Digby. The portrait drawing by Isaac Oliver of an *Unknown Boy, formerly called Henry, Prince of Wales*, was also displayed separately in the gallery.

By 1862 the duke had acquired the core of his collection of historical miniatures. Many of the finest of these were shown in the great exhibition of portraits held that year at the recently founded South Kensington Museum. A major selection was also shown there three years after in the exhibition devoted to portrait miniatures.[5] Since then selections from the Buccleuch miniatures have been lent regularly to specialist exhibitions around the world.

It is also worth noting that after Walter Francis's death in 1884, his son William, 6th Duke of Buccleuch and 8th Duke of Queensberry (1831–1914), added to the collection of portrait miniatures by making a number of significant purchases. Most important was the acquisition of Holbein's limning of *George Neville, 3rd Baron Abergavenny*, for which he paid Colnaghi's to bid up to £430.10s at the Earl of Westmorland's sale in 1892. The 6th Duke also acquired at least two works by Hilliard, as well as seventeenth-century examples by Hoskins, Samuel Cooper, Flatman and Gibson. From the eighteenth century he acquired enamels by Jeremiah Meyer of Benjamin Franklin and by Henry Spicer of Margaret Poyntz, Countess Spencer. It is also significant that the 6th Duke commissioned Andrew McKay, who worked at Colnaghi's, to compile a catalogue of the Buccleuch collection of miniatures, which was privately printed in 1896, with a second and more detailed edition following three years later.[6]

It was William's son, John, 7th Duke of Buccleuch and 9th Duke of Queensberry (1864–1935), who, in 1916, during the First World War, lent virtually the whole collection to the Victoria & Albert Museum, where it remained on public view for four years. From the mid-nineteenth century the miniatures were displayed in the family's London home at Montagu House in Whitehall (built 1853–9), which the 5th Duke had commissioned from the architect William Burn. However, just before the outbreak of the First World War the family and the miniatures moved to Grosvenor Place, also in London. During the Second World War the collection of miniatures was unharmed, although around fifteen of the finest of the sixteenth and seventeenth-century miniatures were sold to British art museums and galleries.[7] After the war the collection was brought to Scotland, where many of the miniatures were displayed at Drumlanrig in large Victorian frames, either in the corridors or on easels in the dining room [fig.3]. In recent decades a selection of the finest miniatures has been exhibited to the public in the Italian room at Bowhill in the Scottish Borders.[8]

NOTES AND REFERENCES

1. Edinburgh 1996–7, especially pp.15–22, and see bibliography, pp.107–11.

2. *ODNB* 2004, XLIX, pp.512–13, entry by K.D. Reynolds; Fraser 1878, I, pp.513–25. Today although the Buccleuch estates have been reduced to almost half their size compared with the 1880s, they are now the most extensive to be held privately in Britain, see Cannadine 1990, p.710.

3. For Sir Walter Scott as a collector and creator of Romantic antiquarian interiors at Abbotsford, see Wainwright 1989, pp.147–207 and Brown 2003, *passim*.

4. Edinburgh 1996–7, p.97.

5. London 1865.

6. McKay 1899.

7. Edinburgh 1996–7, pp.98–9.

8. For the previous history of the Buccleuch miniatures, see London 1916–20, Kennedy 1917, Wood 1917. For the display of the miniatures at Montagu House, see McKay 1899 and Murdoch 1992, pp.12–13, fig.1; at Drumlanrig, see Girouard 1960, III, pp.490–1, fig.6. I am most grateful to the Duke and Duchess of Buccleuch for their assistance in my research, and also for their permission to quote from the archival sources at Bowhill.

COLOUR PLATES

PLATE 1 · CATALOGUE 2

JOHN HOSKINS

*Self-portrait (c.1590–1664/5) c.*1620, on recto; *Self-portrait drawing with five other heads*, on verso

Bodycolour on vellum, set in nineteenth-century gilt-metal locket; 6.9cm (2¾in) high; signed in gold on recto in monogram: *IH*; inscribed on verso in pen and ink: *J Hoskins by / himself*; cartouche engraved: *JOHN HOSKINS*.
ENGRAVED: in stipple by George Perfect Harding in 1802
COLLECTIONS: probably acquired by Walter Francis, 5th Duke of Buccleuch and 7th Duke of Queensberry; by family descent
REFERENCES: McKay 1899, p.15, no.25; Kennedy 1917, pp.14 and 33, pl.XXVI; Long 1929, p.225; Murdoch 1997, pp.43–5; *ODNB* 2004
EXHIBITED: London 1974, p.76, no.142, ills.

On the front of this unusual self-portrait John Hoskins (c.1590–1664/5) shows himself in profile against a darkened background and wearing an open-necked white shirt. The intriguing drawing on the back also represents Hoskins, probably with members of his family including his wife and children, as well as possibly his two nephews and pupils, the miniaturists Samuel and Alexander Cooper. Another self-portrait by Hoskins, almost in profile and in crayons, was noted by the eighteenth-century antiquarian Horace Walpole as having been in the collection of the late seventeenth-century miniaturist Peter Cross, though this work has remained untraced.

Together with his contemporary Peter Oliver (1589–1647), John Hoskins was the most significant miniaturist working in London after the deaths of Isaac Oliver in 1617 and Nicholas Hilliard in 1619, and prior to the emergence of Samuel Cooper in the early 1640s. His earliest miniatures are painted in the tradition of his famous predecessors, while his early work is strongly influenced by the oil painter William Larkin. During the later 1620s and throughout the 1630s, like Peter Oliver, Hoskins worked for Charles I.

It is unclear yet to what degree Hoskins's son, known as John Hoskins the Younger and born sometime between 1617 and 1630, had a separate artistic identity from his father.

IN THE COLLECTION OF THE DUKE OF BUCCLEUCH AND QUEENSBERRY KT

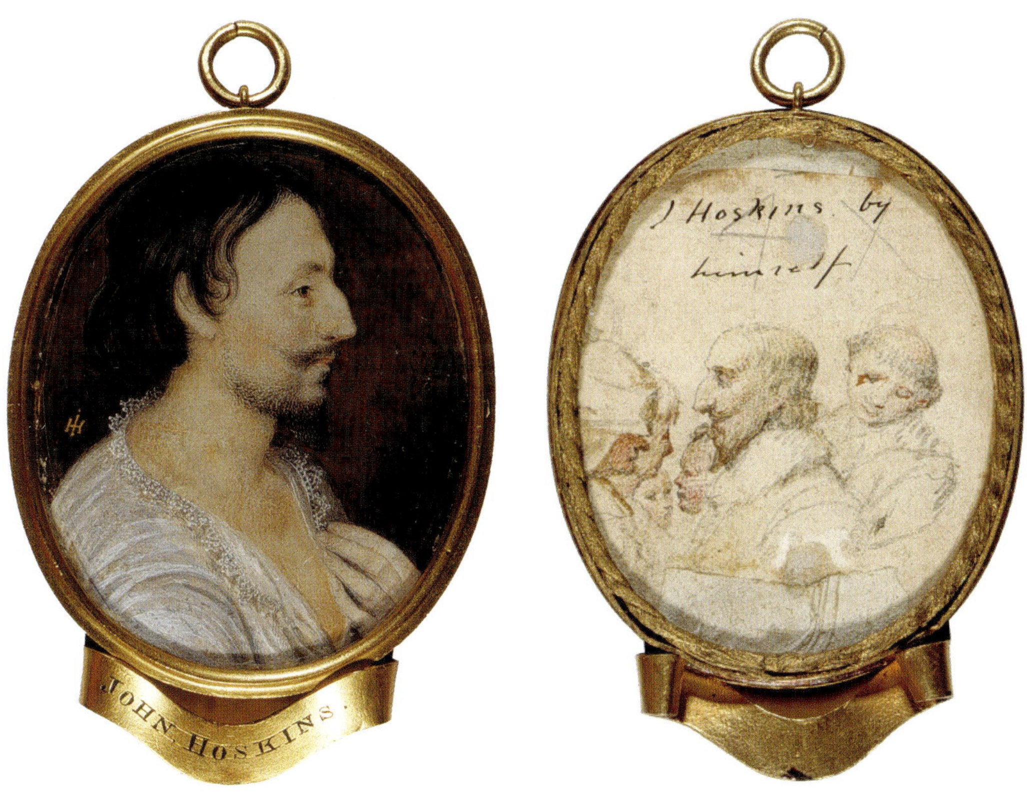
HH
JOHN. HOSKINS.
J Hoskins by
himself

PLATE 2 · CATALOGUE 5

JOHN HOSKINS

Lady Mary Villiers, later Lady Herbert, and later Duchess of Lennox and Richmond (1622–1685) c.1636

Bodycolour on vellum stuck to plain card, set in square early eighteenth-century 'Lens' ebonised wooden frame; 5.1cm (2in) high; painted in gold on recto of frame: *The Dutchess of Richmond.*; inscribed on verso in pencil on paper: *The / Dutchess / of Richmond*; carved into back of frame: *33*

COLLECTIONS: The Dukes of Hamilton; by family descent to Lady Susan Douglas-Hamilton (d.1755), who married Anthony Tracy-Keck of Great Tew (1712–1767); their eldest daughter, Henrietta Charlotte, Viscountess Hereford (1742–1817); her sister Susan, Lady Elcho; by family descent.

REFERENCES: Barnes *et al.* 2004, pp.589–90, no.IV.204, col. pl.; Marshall 1973, p.45

This miniature is a variant by Hoskins of Sir Anthony van Dyck's full-length portrait in oils of the sitter, together with her cousin Charles Hamilton, Earl of Arran as Cupid, which was painted around 1636 for James, 3rd Marquess and later 1st Duke of Hamilton (now in the North Carolina Museum of Art, Raleigh). In the oil painting the sitter wears similar pearls (which have oxidised and turned black in the miniature) and an identical fur wrap. Van Dyck shows the sitter standing against a colonnade and neutral sky background, but in the miniature Hoskins presents her in front of a vividly-coloured sky, set in a landscape with buildings over her right shoulder. In the oil she looks directly out at the viewer, while in the miniature she looks out to her right.

The sitter was the daughter of George Villiers, 1st Duke of Buckingham, the favourite of James VI & I. She was first married in 1635 to Charles, Lord Herbert, heir to his father, the 4th Earl of Pembroke. Lord Herbert died the following year, and the portraits by Van Dyck and Hoskins were most probably painted to mark that event. In 1637 she married James Stuart, 4th Duke of Lennox and 1st Duke of Richmond, her second marriage. Her third marriage was in 1664 to Colonel Thomas Howard. In later life she was a Lady of the Bedchamber to Charles II's queen, Catherine of Braganza.

THE EARL OF WEMYSS AND MARCH KT

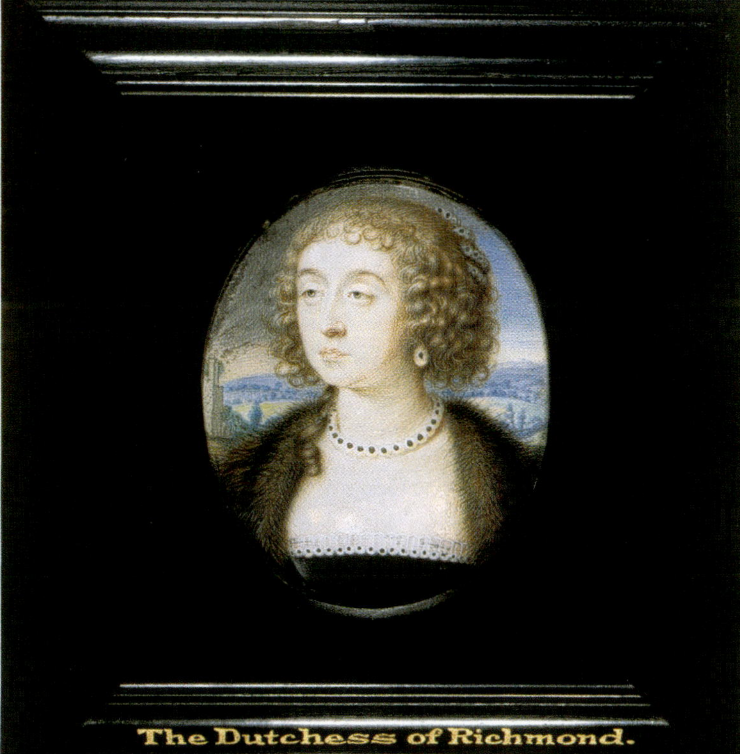
The Dutchess of Richmond.

PLATE 3 · CATALOGUE 7

SAMUEL COOPER

*Sir Charles Compton (c.1623–1661) c.*1645–50

Bodycolour on vellum, set in gold locket frame; 6.3cm (2½in) high; scratched on verso: *Sir Charles Compton*
COLLECTIONS: by family descent

The sitter was the second son of Spencer Compton, 2nd Earl of Northampton, an ardent royalist in the Civil War who fought at the Battle of Edgehill in 1642 and was killed in action during the engagement at Hopton Heath the following year. After Edgehill and the king's return to Oxford he knighted four of the 2nd Earl's sons, including the sitter. The king also gave the 2nd Earl responsibility for the region around Banbury and commanded him to raise a regiment of horse, over which Sir Charles Compton was made Lieutenant-Colonel. A similar head-and-shoulders oil portrait was in the collection of the Marquess of Northampton in 1842, when it was reproduced as a hand-coloured lithograph in the *Histories of Noble British Families*, published in London by William Pickering in 1842.

Samuel Cooper (?1608–1672) was the finest miniaturist working in London during the seventeenth century, and can also be considered one of the outstanding European portraitists of his generation. After leaving the home of John Hoskins, his uncle and tutor, he appears to have travelled on the Continent. He re-established himself in London in 1641–2, and produced a steady output of miniatures throughout the rest of his career. Such was his reputation that he was in demand from both Royalist and Parliamentarian sitters in the 1640s, and he continued his successful practice under the Commonwealth and the Restoration. In 1663 Charles II appointed him as King's Limner with an annual salary of £200. An accomplished musician and linguist, Cooper's studio was a focal point of London society during the middle decades of the seventeenth century. His younger brother, Alexander Cooper (1609–*c.*1660) was also a limner.

PRIVATE COLLECTION

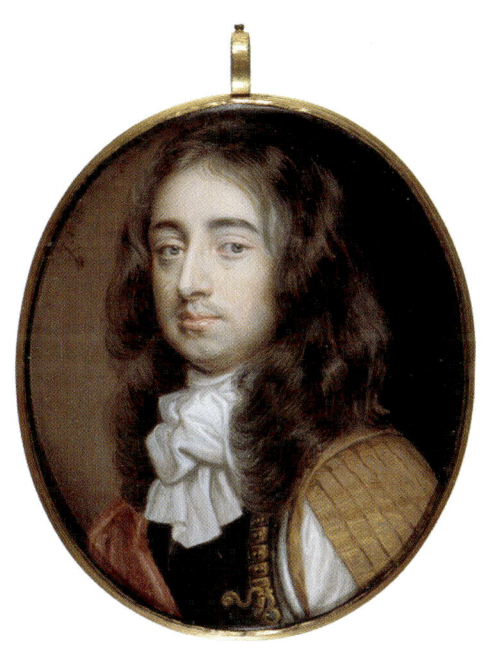

PLATE 4 · CATALOGUE 17

RICHARD GIBSON AFTER SIR PETER LELY

*Elizabeth Wriothesley, Lady Percy, later Countess of Northumberland (1645/6–1690) c.*1665–70

Bodycolour on vellum, set in later nineteenth-century gilt-metal frame; 6.5cm (2½in) high; inscribed on a piece of paper on the verso in a later hand: *The Mother of his Grace / ye Duke of Montagu / Mas.tr of the most Hon.ble / Order of the Bath / N: Gibson*; and in another hand: *Eliazbeth Countess / of Northumberland / Boughton House, 12/18*; engraved on cartouche: *ELIZ. COUNTESS OF NORTHUMBERLAND*

COLLECTIONS: by family descent

REFERENCES: McKay 1899, p.102, no.6; Kennedy 1917, pp.23–4; Murdoch *et al.* 1981, p.133, pl.144

EXHIBITED: London 1974, p.98, no.186, ill.; London & New Haven 2001–2, p.108, no.27, col. pl.

The sitter was the youngest daughter of Thomas Wriothesley, 4th Earl of Southampton. She married Joceline Percy, who in 1668 became the 11th Earl of Northumberland, and on his death in 1670 inherited a great fortune. Her second marriage was to Ralph, 1st Duke of Montagu in 1673. She died at Boughton House in Northamptonshire, and the Montagu estate now belongs to the Duke of Buccleuch.

This miniature is one of Gibson's copies 'in little' from an oil portrait of the sitter made by Sir Peter Lely, one of the set of 'Windsor Beauties' that is now at Hampton Court. A related composition by Lely, though of lesser quality, is at Boughton.

Until 1981 the study of miniatures by Richard Gibson (1615–1690) was beset with confusion over the mythical figure of David Gibson. After studying with Francis Cleyn at the Mortlake tapestry works, Gibson was appointed a page to Charles I. In 1640/1 he married another dwarf at court, Anne Sheppard. After Samuel Cooper's death in 1672 he was appointed King's Limner, an appointment he held for only one year before he was succeeded by Nicholas Dixon. Among his five surviving children was the miniaturist Susannah-Penelope Rosse (*c.*1655–1690).

IN THE COLLECTION OF THE DUKE OF BUCCLEUCH AND QUEENSBERRY KT

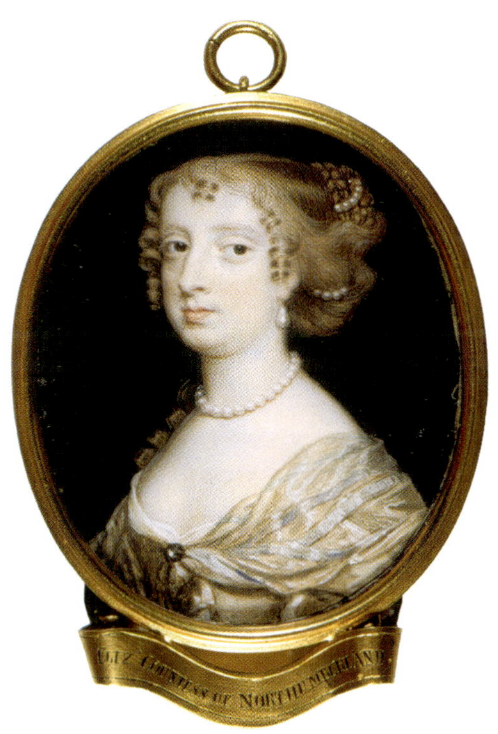
ELIZ COUNTESS OF NORTHUMBERLAND

PLATE 5 · CATALOGUE 22

DAVID LOGGAN

Edward Nicholas (b.1624 – after 1672) 1672

Plumbago on vellum, set in turned wooden frame; 12cm (4¾in) high; signed and dated at lower right: DL *fect / 1672*; inscribed in pen and ink on verso: *Edward Nicholas / 1672*
COLLECTIONS: by family descent
REFERENCES: *ODNB 2004*

The artist and engraver David Loggan (1634–1692) was born in Danzig, Poland, where he was baptised in the Calvinist church. He was the only son of the merchant John Loggan, whose family was of Scottish ancestry and had settled in Oxfordshire during the sixteenth century, and his wife, Margaret, the widow of John or Johann Klinge. Loggan studied with engraver Hondius in Danzig and after the latter's death in 1652 with Crispijn de Passe in Amsterdam. He settled in London between 1656 and 1658 and drew a pencil portrait of Oliver Cromwell before his death. In the early 1660s Loggan made a reputation for his highly sensitive small portrait drawings drawn from life in plumbago or lead point on vellum, and he succeeded William Faithorne as the leading portrait draughtsman working on this small scale. From 1665 to 1675 he was in Oxford, where he undertook portrait commissions and engraved views of the colleges in the University for *Oxonia illustrata* (1675) in a style that was heavily influenced by the prints of Wenceslaus Hollar. When he moved back to London he continued to draw and engrave portraits, and acted as an agent for the portraitist Sir Peter Lely. His views of the Cambridge colleges were published as *Cantabrigia illustrata* (1690).

The sitter was the second son of Sir Edward Nicholas, who was Secretary of State to both Charles I and Charles II, and of his wife, Jane, third daughter of Henry Jay of Holston, Norfolk, who was an alderman in the city of London.

PRIVATE COLLECTION

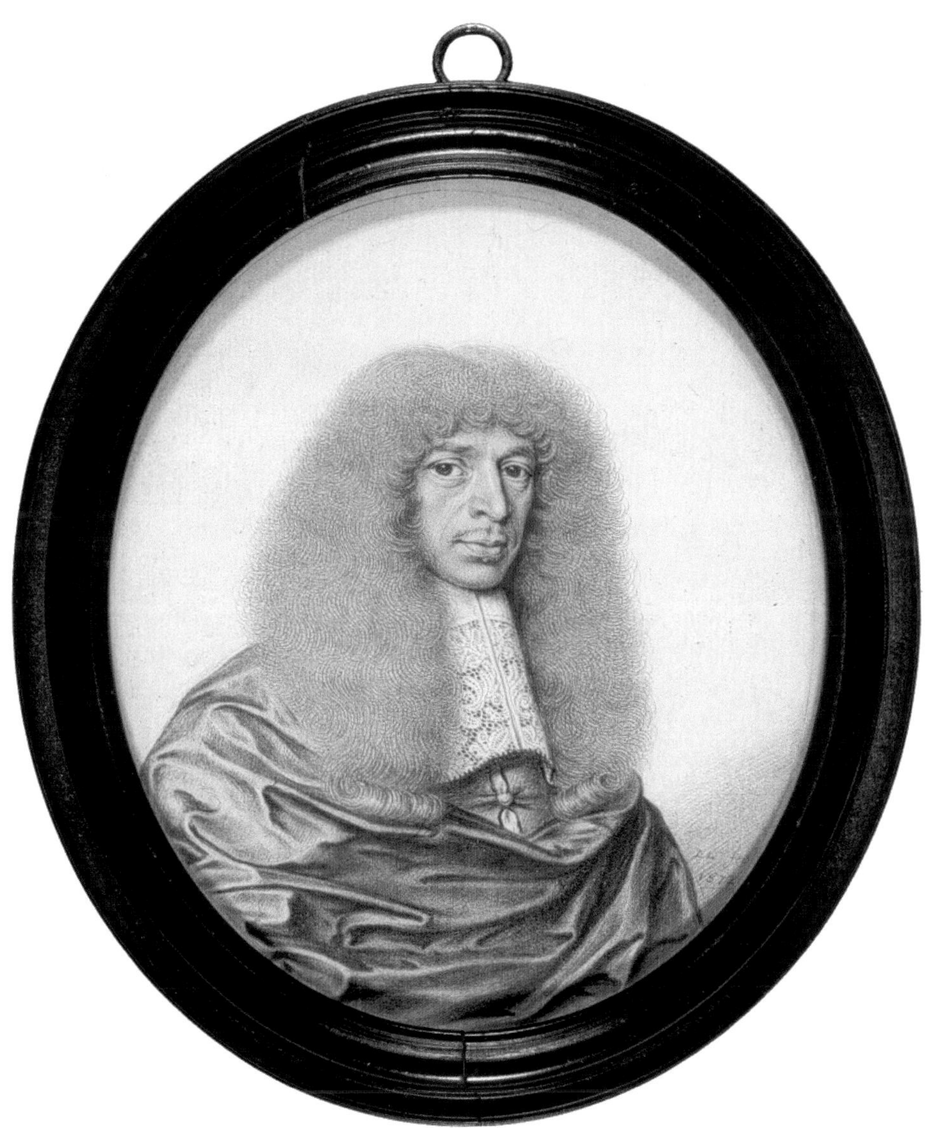

PLATE 6 · CATALOGUE 23

W.P. (POSSIBLY WILLIAM PAWLETT)

Mary Davis (fl.1660 – after 1698) c.1673

Bodycolour on vellum, set in nineteenth-century gilt-metal frame; 8.3cm (3¼in) high; signed on recto at lower left with initials: *WP*; cartouche engraved: *NELL GWYNNE.*
COLLECTIONS: probably acquired by Walter Francis, 5th Duke of Buccleuch; by family descent
REFERENCES: McKay 1899, p.122, no.34; Kennedy 1917, p.28, pl.LIII; Murdoch 1997, p.303
EXHIBITED: London and New Haven 2001–2, pp.155–6, col. pl. and p.241

The actress Mary 'Moll' Davis was one of Charles II's mistresses in the late 1660s and early 1670s, and she probably bore him a daughter in 1673, known as Lady Mary Tudor. Details of her early life are not known, though she may have been an illegitimate daughter of Thomas Howard, Earl of Berkshire. She was an actress in the King's Company from 1660 to 1668, whereupon she became the king's mistress. Mary Davis performed in the court masques *Calisto* (1675) and *Venus and Adonis* (1681–2). In 1686 she married the court musician James Paisible. The couple went into exile in France in 1688 but returned to England in 1698.

This three-quarter length miniature is almost certainly based on an untraced oil portrait of Mary Davis by Sir Peter Lely. It was erroneously thought in the nineteenth century to be of the king's most famous mistress, Nell Gwyn. The identity of the miniaturist who signed his miniatures WP is not known. However, one possibility is William Pawlett (fl.1661– after 1701), who was appointed 'Lymner in Ordinary for Drawing & Coppying of Pictures for his Mats. Cabinett' in 1673.

IN THE COLLECTION OF THE DUKE OF BUCCLEUCH AND QUEENSBERRY KT

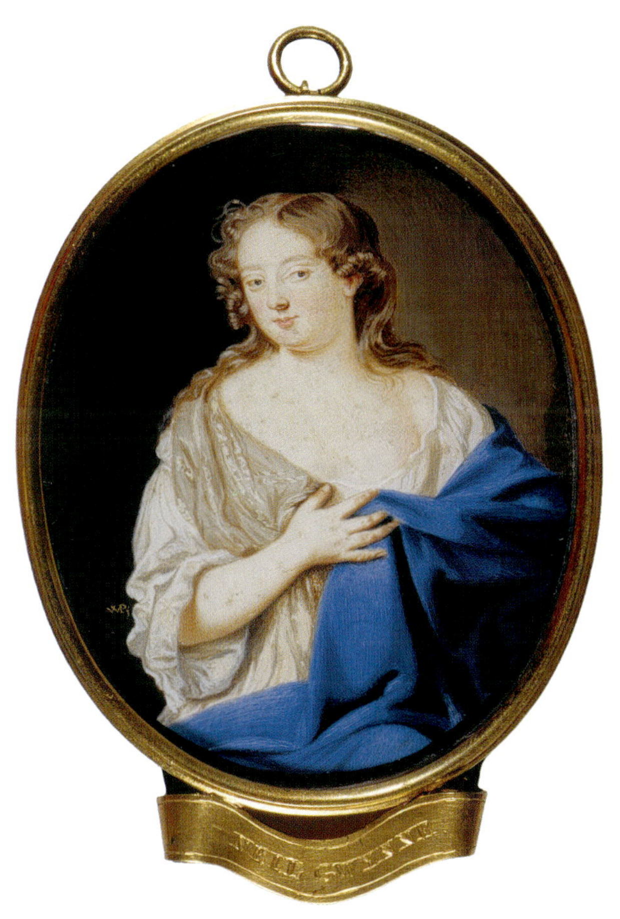
NELL GWYNNE

PLATE 7 · CATALOGUE 32

BERNARD LENS III AFTER SIR GODFREY KNELLER

*James Douglas, Earl of Arran, later 4th Duke of Hamilton (1658–1712) c.*1712

Bodycolour on vellum, set in original ebonised 'Lens' wooden frame; 21.6 × 13.9cm (8½ × 5½in) high; signed and dated in gold on recto at lower left with monogram: *BL*; gilt-metal cartouche engraved: *JAMES / 4TH DUKE OF HAMILTON*; pen and ink inscription on verso: *The Duke of Hamilton my grandfather [——] 1712 held a duel with Lord Mohun who fell by his hand and his second Col. Macartney murdered the Duke [——] painted by Lens & thought most valuable / L.F. Elcho*

COLLECTIONS: The sitter's daughter, Lady Susan Douglas-Hamilton (d.1755), who married Anthony Tracy-Keck of Great Tew (1712–1767); their eldest daughter Henrietta Charlotte, Viscountess Hereford (1742–1817); her sister Susan, Lady Elcho (1745–1835); by family descent

REFERENCES: Coombs 1998, pp.80–3; Marshall 1973, *passim*, especially pp.228–9

The sitter was the eldest son of Anne, Duchess of Hamilton in her own right, who in 1656 married William Douglas, 1st Earl of Selkirk and later 3rd Duke of Hamilton. The 4th Duke was an opponent of the Act of Union in 1707, but four years later Queen Anne further ennobled him as Duke of Brandon. A year later she made him a Knight of the Garter and appointed him ambassador to France. However, before he could travel to Paris, he quarrelled with Lord Mohun, which led to a duel in Hyde Park on 13 November 1712. The duke ran Mohun through with his sword, but before dying he managed to sever an artery in the duke's right arm, thus killing him a few moments later. The original full-length portrait of the 4th Duke by Kneller, still belongs to his descendants and hangs at Lennoxlove House in East Lothian.

Bernard Lens III (1682–1740), who was the son and grandson of two rather obscure artists of the same name, was the first miniaturist in Britain to make a career working on ivory when it was introduced as a support for painting in watercolour during the first few decades of the eighteenth century. A successful drawing master, Lens worked in a number of the great English country houses. His sons Andrew Benjamin and Peter Paul were both miniature painters.

THE EARL OF WEMYSS AND MARCH KT

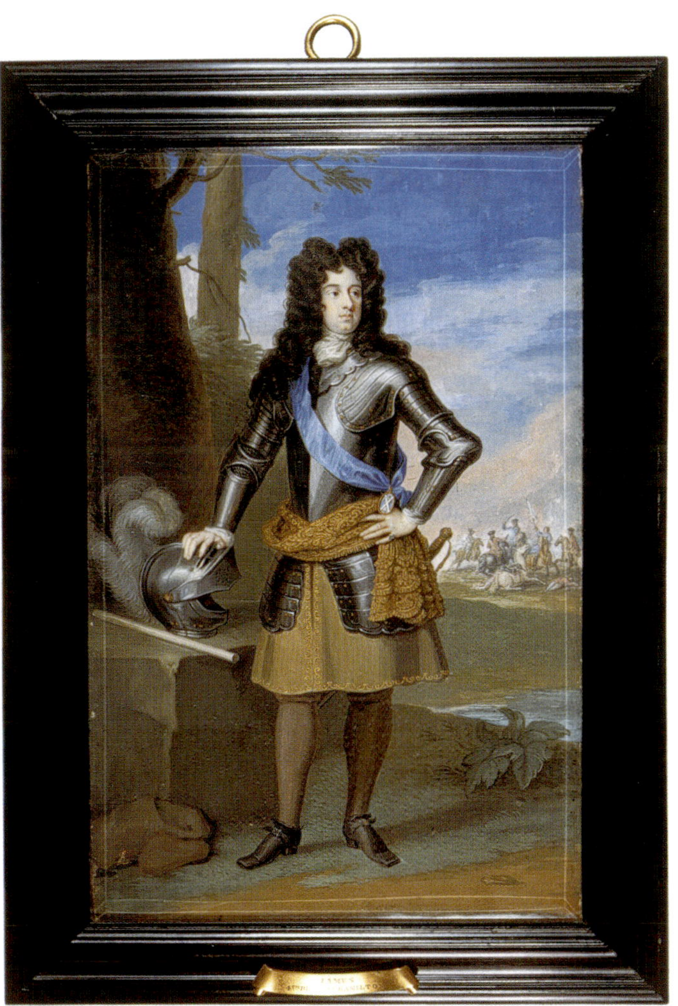

PLATE 8 · CATALOGUE 36

WILLIAM PREWETT

Horatio (or Horace) Walpole, 4th Earl of Orford (1717–1797) 1735

Enamel on copper, set in gilt-metal frame; 4.5cm (1¾in) high; signed and dated on counter enamel: *W. Prewett pinx / 1735*; gilt-metal cartouche engraved: *HORACE WALPOLE. / BY PREWETT.*
COLLECTIONS: probably acquired by Walter Francis, 5th Duke of Buccleuch; by family descent
REFERENCES: McKay 1899, p.96, no.31; Kennedy 1917, pp.28 and 43, pl.LXVII; Foster 1926, p.243; Long 1929, p.351; *ODNB* 2004
EXHIBITED: London 1934, no.986; Edinburgh 1965, no.391, pl.96

Horatio, or Horace, Walpole was the fourth son of the famous prime minister, Sir Robert Walpole, 1st Earl of Orford, by his first wife Catherine Shorter. He was a famous author, wit, letter-writer and virtuoso, perhaps best known for his Gothic romance *The Castle of Otranto* (1764), and for creating Strawberry Hill, a villa on the river Thames at Twickenham that he referred to as his 'little Gothic castle'. This he filled with his library and collections of oil portraits, sculpture, armour, china, curiosities, objets d'art, as well as a highly important collection of enamels and miniatures. The collections of this celebrated connoisseur and antiquarian were sold in a spectacular auction in 1842. A considerable group of the miniatures and enamels were either acquired at the sale for Walter Francis, 5th Duke of Buccleuch, or found their way into his collection over the following decades.

Little is known of the enamellist William Prewett (fl.1735–6), except that he may have been born in Suffolk, and is likely to have been a pupil of Christian Friedrich Zincke, one of the leading enamellists working in Britain during the first half of the eighteenth century. Enamels by Prewett are scarce, but there are two examples in the Victoria & Albert Museum, London: that of Mr and Mrs John Knight with Mr Newsham is signed and dated 1735 on the front, while that of Mr Newsham on his own is signed and dated 1736 on the counter enamel.

IN THE COLLECTION OF THE DUKE OF BUCCLEUCH AND QUEENSBERRY KT

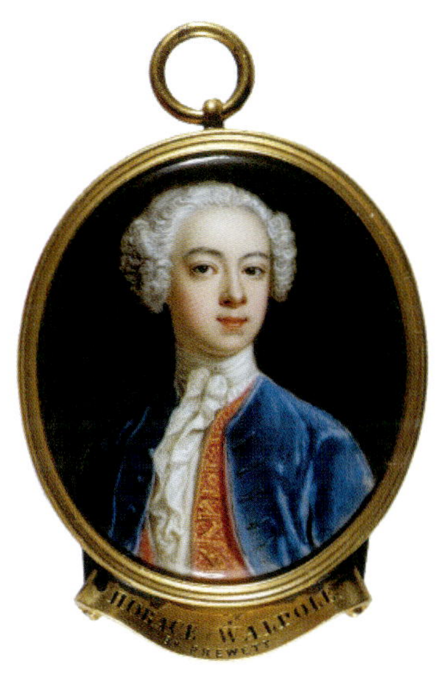
HORACE WALPOLE
BY PREWETT

PLATE 9 · CATALOGUE 41

JEAN-ANDRE ROUQUET

James Drummond, 6th Earl and 3rd titular Duke of Perth (1713–1746) c.1740

Enamel on copper, set in elaborate gold frame with panels of blue enamel within lines of white, set with the initial *P* and sprays of leaves in diamond sparks; 4.5cm (1⅞in) high; engraved on verso: *James Duke of Perth*
COLLECTIONS: by family descent
EXHIBITED: Glasgow 1888; London 1889, no.253–19

The sitter was the eldest son of James Drummond, 5th Earl and 2nd titular Duke of Perth [28, 31], by his wife Lady Jean Gordon. After his father's death in 1716, he was sent to France where he was educated at the Scotch College in Douai and later in Paris. In 1731 he returned to his ancestral estates in Scotland, where his father's attainder had deprived him of a legal title. At the start of the Jacobite Rebellion of 1745, he escaped arrest and joined Prince Charles Edward Stuart at Perth in September of that year. The following year he commanded the left wing of the Jacobite forces at the Battle of Culloden, where he was wounded. Rescued by the French frigate *La Bellone*, he died on board on 13 May 1746, and his body was committed to the deep.

Jean-André Rouquet (1701–1758) was born in Geneva into a family of French Huguenot refugees. By the mid-1720s he had moved to London, where he worked as an enameller – in the style of Boit and Zincke – for the next thirty years. Rouquet was a friend of Hogarth, whose enamel portrait he painted in around 1745 (National Portrait Gallery, London). He moved to Paris in 1753, and was allocated a studio in the Palais du Louvre the following year, when he was elected a member of the Académie Royale. Rouquet exhibited his work at the Salon between 1753 and 1757. He published *L'Etat des Arts en Angleterre* in Paris during 1755, which was also translated and published that same year in London as *The Present State of the Arts in England*. This included a comprehensive guide to the English market and fashion for portraiture. Rouquet died in 1758 at the asylum for the insane at Charenton, near Paris.

PRIVATE COLLECTION

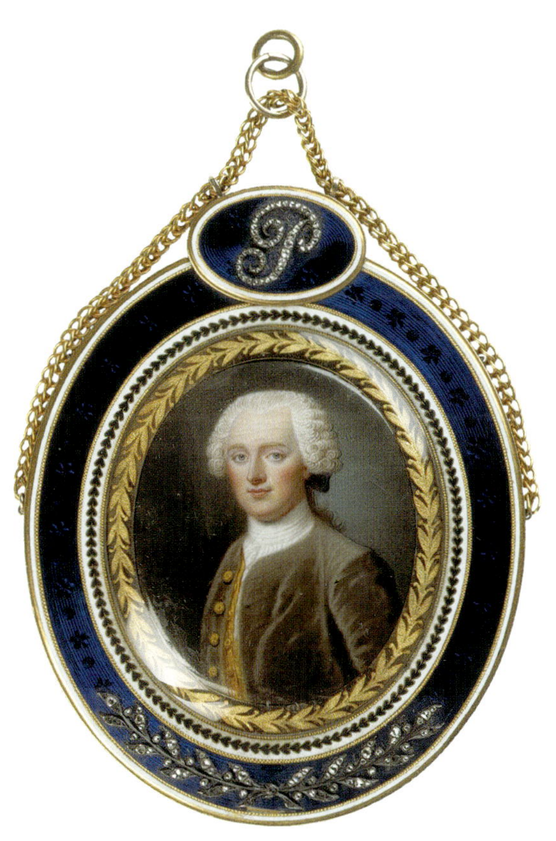

PLATE 10 · CATALOGUE 42

JEAN-ETIENNE LIOTARD

Maria Theresa, Empress of Austria (1717–1780) 1743

Bodycolour and watercolour on vellum; 3.6cm (1½in) high; set inside of main gold locket, with a mirror facing set underneath larger opening lid

JEAN-ETIENNE LIOTARD

Duchess Maria Anna (1718–1744) 1744

Bodycolour and watercolour on vellum; 5.1cm (2in) high, set on outside of larger opening lid of gold locket

JEAN-ANDRE ROUQUET

*Miss Anne Murray Keith (1736–1818) c.*1745

enamel on copper; 3.6cm (1½in) high, set inside smaller opening lid of gold locket

COLLECTIONS: locket probably presented to Robert Keith (*c.*1697–1774); to his daughter Anne Murray Keith; by family descent

REFERENCES: Loche & Roethlisberger 1978, pp.93–5, no.58 and 69, ills.; Walker 1992, pp.262–3; *ODNB* 2004

This gold locket, which was probably made in Vienna during the mid-1740s, contains three portraits. The two by Liotard were almost certainly made just before the death of the Austrian Duchess Maria Anna in 1744, the year of her marriage to Charles of Lorraine. She was the younger sister of Maria Theresa, who in 1740 had succeeded her father as Archduchess of Austria, Queen of Hungary and Bohemia, and Holy Roman Empress. This miniature of Maria Theresa is closely related to one of Liotard's earliest portraits of the empress, a pastel of 1743 which was formerly in the collection of Max, Duke of Hohenberg, in Vienna. The miniature of the Duchess Maria Anna is a variant of the Liotard pastel of her dated 1744, which is now in the Schlossmuseum at Weimar. The enamel of Anne Murray Keith was painted by Rouquet in London. Her father, Robert Keith, was the only son of Colonel Robert Keith of Craig, Kincardineshire, and Agnes, daughter of Robert Murray of Murrayshall, Stirlingshire. Keith was appointed British minister at Vienna in 1748, and served there until 1757.

PRIVATE COLLECTION

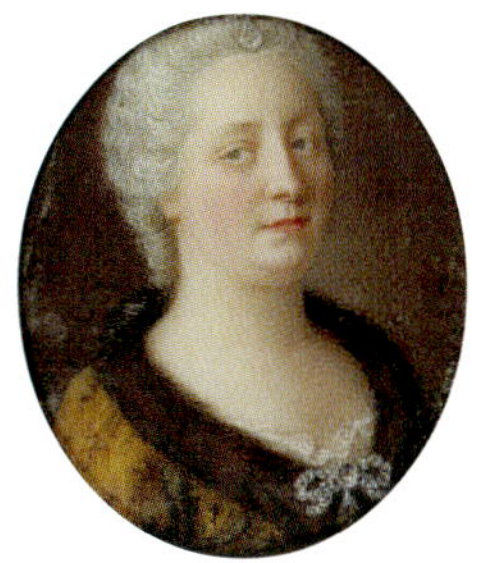

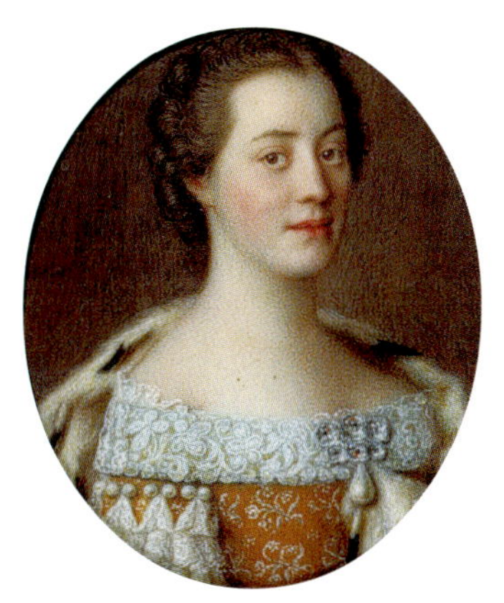

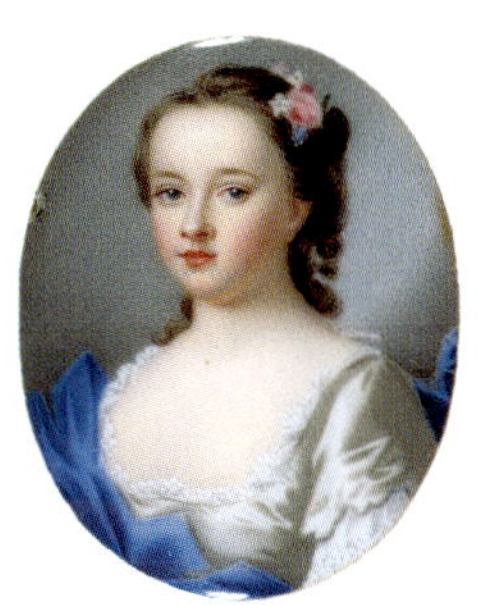

PLATE 11 · CATALOGUE 43

JOHN DANIEL KAMM AFTER MAURICE-QUENTIN DE LA TOUR

*Prince Charles Edward Stuart (1720–1788) c.*1749–50

Bodycolour and watercolour on vellum, set in gilt-metal frame; 6.4cm (2½in) high
COLLECTIONS: D.S. Lavender (Antiques) Ltd, London
REFERENCES: Nicholas 1973, pp.34–5 and p.28 col. pl.; Walker 1992, p.40, no.82, ill.; Edinburgh 1996–7, p.94, no.67, ill.; Edinburgh 2001, pp.97–8
EXHIBITED: London 1993, no.83, col. pl.

Prince Charles Edward Stuart was the eldest son of Prince James Francis Edward Stuart ('The Old Pretender') and Princess Maria Clementina Sobieska. Having been born in Rome and spent his whole early life on the Continent, Prince Charles returned to Scotland for the ill-fated Jacobite Rising of 1745, which ended with the calamitous Battle of Culloden the following year. After a few years in France, he spent the rest of his life in Italy.

This miniature is a fine example of the many copies taken from the famous pastel portrait of the Young Pretender by Maurice-Quentin de La Tour (1702–1788), which was made and exhibited in Paris during 1748, and was purchased by the Scottish National Portrait Gallery in 1994. Another rectangular copy of the La Tour portrait by Kamm, which is signed and dated ('J. Kamm / 1750') was in the Donald Nicholas collection in 1972. An oval version painted on card, most probably by Kamm, is in the Royal Collection at Windsor Castle. Similar copies were painted by the Orcadian Jacobite, Sir Robert Strange (1721–1792), such as the signed oval version in the collection of the Duke of Buccleuch. Very little is known about the miniaturist Kamm (fl.1749–50), except that he was copying the La Tour portrait of Prince Charles Edward Stuart, presumably in Paris, during 1749 and 1750.

PRIVATE COLLECTION

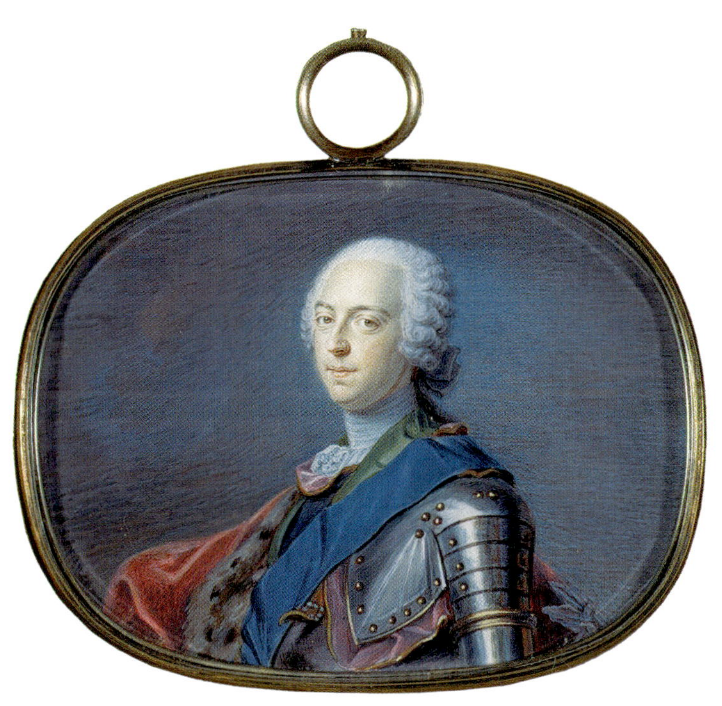

PLATE 12 · CATALOGUE 55

SIR HENRY RAEBURN

*James Gilliland (fl.1730–90) c.*1775

Watercolour on ivory (cracked; conserved in 1998), set in gilt-metal frame; 5.1 cm high (2in)
COLLECTIONS: by family descent
REFERENCES: Milner 1997; Edinburgh and London 1997–8, p.202; Zachs 1998, pl.2ab (left); Edinburgh 2004, pp.50–1, col. pl. and pp.107–8
EXHIBITED: Edinburgh and London 1997–8 (London only); Edinburgh 1999, p.57, no.26, col. ill.

This miniature is a rare early surviving portrait in watercolour on ivory by the eminent Scottish oil painter, Sir Henry Raeburn (1756–1823). It is paired with the portrait miniature by Raeburn of Gilliland's wife, Elizabeth MacMurray [56]. The Gilliland portraits can be compared to the miniatures by Raeburn of the etcher and seal engraver, David Deuchar (National Gallery of Scotland), dated 1773; of *George Sandilands of Strathtyrum* [58], which can be dated to around 1775; and of *Andrew Wood* [57], datable to the later 1770s. Two portrait drawings of unknown gentlemen by Raeburn, which are studies for his miniatures, have been discovered recently in the print room of the National Gallery of Scotland, where they had been previously thought to be by John Brown.

James Gilliland was a jeweller and goldsmith, working in the luckenbooths in Edinburgh's Parliament Square. On 21 October 1771 an arrangement was made between Raeburn's school, George Heriot's Hospital, and Gilliland his future master. The indenture of Raeburn as an apprentice to Gilliland was made on 27 June 1772.

JOHN MURRAY

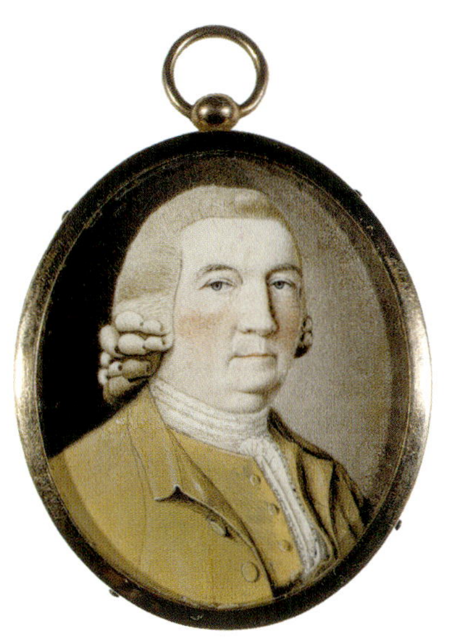

PLATE 13 · CATALOGUE 59

RICHARD COSWAY

Francis Charteris of Amisfield, later 7th Earl of Wemyss (1725–1809) 1779

Watercolour on ivory, set in locket decorated with gold, diamonds, Bristol glass and enamel; on the verso a hair setting and earl's coronet over monogram in diamonds CW, with original closing red leather case; 4.3cm (1¾in) high
COLLECTIONS: by family descent
REFERENCES: Gosford House, Muniment Room, 7th Earl of Wemyss's account book, entry for 1779 ('Rich. Cosway picture of myself and setting it in gold £17/17'); Lloyd 2005, p.48, no.8, col. pl.
EXHIBITED: Edinburgh 1999, p.58, no.30, and p.13, fig.4

It is likely that this splendid diamond and enamelled setting was added to Cosway's earlier miniature when Francis Charteris of Amisfield became the 7th Earl of Wemyss in 1787. The 7th Earl's account book records that this portrait originally had a gold setting, and that both it and the miniature cost the sitter seventeen guineas in 1779. Eight years earlier, in 1771, the same sitter had sat for a much more modest portrait miniature from Ozias Humphry (1742–1810), one of Cosway's rivals during the 1760s and 1770s, which had cost the sitter twelve guineas.

Richard Cosway (1742–1821) was one of the most fashionable portraitists working in London during the late Georgian and Regency period. After moving from his native Devon to London in 1754, he studied at William Shipley's drawing school, where he won numerous prizes. In 1760 he exhibited for the first time – an oil portrait of his master – at the newly founded Society of Artists. While Cosway also undertook portrait drawings and works in oils, it was as a miniaturist that he found the greatest success. He married the talented Anglo-Italian artist, musician and educationalist Maria Hadfield in 1781. In the previous year Cosway had first portrayed in miniature the young Prince of Wales (later the Prince Regent and George IV), who became his most important patron. Apart from having a reputation as a flamboyant dandy and an eccentric mystic, Cosway was also a notable connoisseur, antiquarian and collector of old master paintings, prints and drawings.

THE EARL OF WEMYSS AND MARCH KT

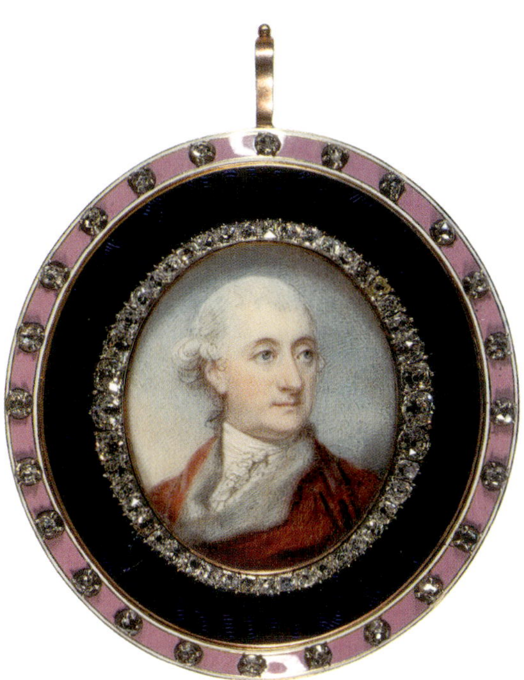

PLATE 14 (RECTO AND VERSO) · CATALOGUE 68

SAMUEL SHELLEY

Douglas Hamilton, 8th Duke of Hamilton and 5th Duke of Brandon (1756–1799) c.1790

Watercolour on ivory, set gold locket frame with verso of Bristol glass and monogram of diamonds *HB* between two diamond sprays and under a ducal coronet of red glass; 7.6cm (3in) high;
COLLECTIONS: by family descent
REFERENCES: Ingamells 1997, pp.446–7

The sitter was the second son of James, 6th Duke of Hamilton, and succeeded his older brother, James, 7th Duke of Hamilton, who had died as a teenager. He spent four years on the Continent between 1772 and 1776 with Dr John Moore as his tutor; the first two years were spent in Geneva, before travelling through Germany to Vienna and across Italy. Their tour was described by Moore in his *View of Society and Manners in Italy* (1781). The 8th Duke was the principal subject of an ambitious Grand Tour portrait by Gavin Hamilton (Scottish National Portrait Gallery, Edinburgh), which was painted in Rome and included his tutor and the latter's son, John (later the hero of the retreat at Corunna in 1809 during the Peninsular War). In 1778 the 8th Duke married Elizabeth Burrell, but they were divorced in 1794. He was made a Knight of the Thistle in 1785.

Samuel Shelley (1756–1808) was born in Whitechapel, London. He entered the Royal Academy schools in 1774 aged seventeen. Awarded a premium by the Society of Arts in 1770, he exhibited at the Society of Artists in 1773 and 1775, and for thirty years at the Royal Academy until 1804. Shelley mainly painted miniatures, but he also made watercolours, drawings and the occasional oil. This miniature of the 8th Duke is one of Shelley's most incisive character studies of a male subject.

IN THE COLLECTION OF LENNOXLOVE HOUSE, HADDINGTON (BY KIND PERMISSION OF THE DUKE OF HAMILTON AND BRANDON)

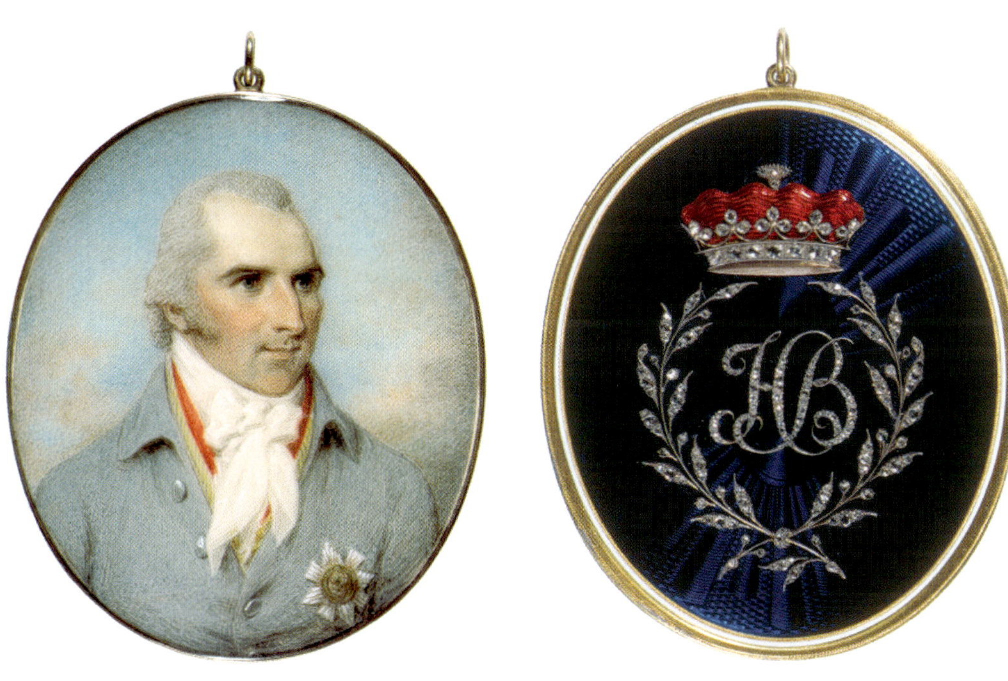
HB

PLATE 15 · CATALOGUE 71

ARCHIBALD SKIRVING

Charles-Philippe, Comte d'Artois, later Charles x (1757–1836) 1796–7

Watercolour on ivory, set into lid of gold and ebonised circular snuffbox, 9cm (3½in) high
COLLECTIONS: gift of Louis-Antoine, Duc d'Angoulême, to Mr Manners
REFERENCES: Lloyd 2005a, p.485, n.58
EXHIBITED: Edinburgh 1951, p.33, no.131; Edinburgh 1999, pp.70–1, no.121

According to a letter (kept inside this snuffbox) which was dated 27 March 1797, and sent from Edinburgh by Louis-Antoine, Duc d'Angoulême to a Mr Manners, the box with the inset miniature was a present from 'Louis Antoine'. He was the eldest son of the sitter, the Comte d'Artois, who was a younger brother of Louis XVI. Charles-Philippe ascended the French throne in 1824 – after the death of his brother Louis XVIII – and reigned as Charles X until his abdication in 1830. During the French Revolution the family were exiled at the Palace of Holyroodhouse in Edinburgh, and the Comte d'Artois stayed there from 1796 to 1803 (Mackenzie-Stuart 1995). The sitter was known as 'Monsieur' and he acclimatised well to life in Edinburgh.

The accompanying letter indicated that the miniature was painted in 1796–7. Archibald Skirving (1749–1819) had only just returned to Edinburgh after a traumatic journey back from his seven-year stay in Italy. This ambitious miniature, confidently painted with diagonal strokes in the background, and with a correct characterisation of the open-mouthed sitter, betrays knowledge of Richard Cosway's miniature style in London. The attribution is supported by comparison with the similar confident handling seen in the 1798 miniatures of James Drummond, Baron Perth [72] and his daughter Clementina Sarah Drummond [73]. Another version of this miniature of the Comte d'Artois is preserved at the Musée Condé at Chantilly (Chantilly 2004, p.58, no.8).

PRIVATE COLLECTION

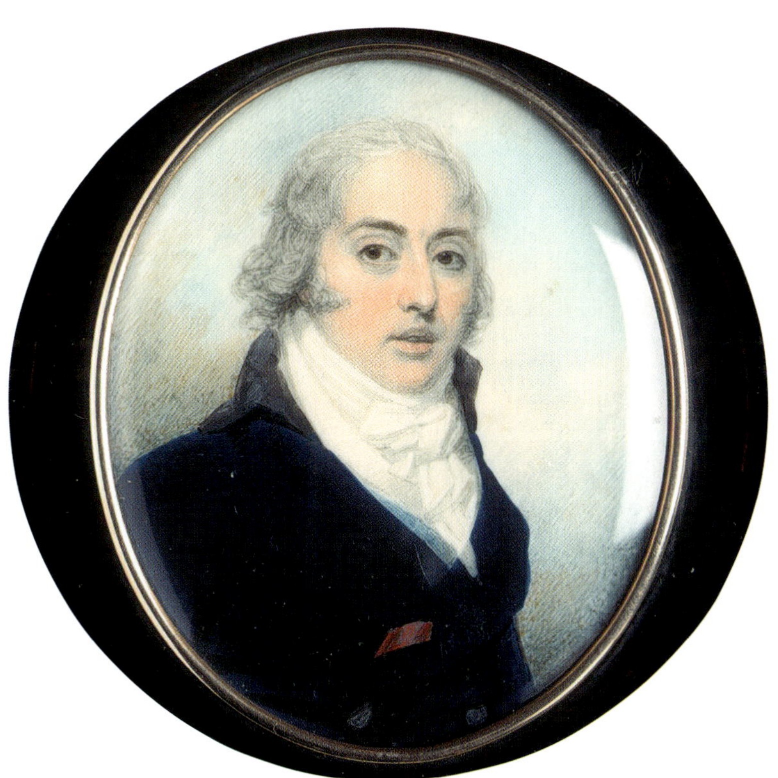

PLATE 16 · CATALOGUE 73

ARCHIBALD SKIRVING

*Clementina Sarah Drummond, later Baroness Willoughby de Eresby (1786–1865) c.*1798

Watercolour on ivory, set in gilt-metal frame; 6.7cm (2⅝in) high; engraved on verso: *Clementina / Lady Willoughby d'Eresby* [*sic*]
COLLECTIONS: by family descent
EXHIBITED: Edinburgh 1999, p.71, no.125 and p.38, col. pl.5

Clementina Sarah Drummond was the daughter and heiress of Captain James Drummond of Lundin, who was made Baron Perth and Lord Drummond of Stobhall in 1797, the year before this miniature and that of the sitter's father [72] were painted by Skirving. The sitter's mother was Clementina Elizabeth, daughter of Charles, 10th Baron Elphinstone [77]. Clementina Sarah is shown wearing a white dress and blue Highland bonnet with black feather, ribbon, bow, streamers and sash of the Drummond tartan. In 1807 Clementina Sarah married Peter Robert Burrell, later 2nd Baron Gwydir and 19th Baron Willoughby de Eresby. She was also portrayed in a miniature by George Sanders (private collection), which can be seen in the background of the cabinet miniature depicting Clementina Sarah's two daughters and painted by Sanders's niece, Christina Robertson [88].

Archibald Skirving was the only significant pastellist to have worked in Scotland during the eighteenth century, with the exception of Catherine Read (1723–1778), who was based in London. After beginning his career in Edinburgh during the early 1770s, Skirving moved to London in 1777, where for seven years he appears to have worked as a miniaturist without much success. After a couple of years back in Edinburgh during the mid-1780s, Skirving travelled to Rome in late 1786, where he studied and practised as a pastellist, miniaturist and draughtsman. On his return to Edinburgh in late 1795 he worked mainly as pastellist, producing painstaking crayon-paintings of the highest quality, before retiring in 1803. Skirving was a notable eccentric, who paid little heed to the conventional norms of behaviour expected of a portraitist in polite society.

PRIVATE COLLECTION

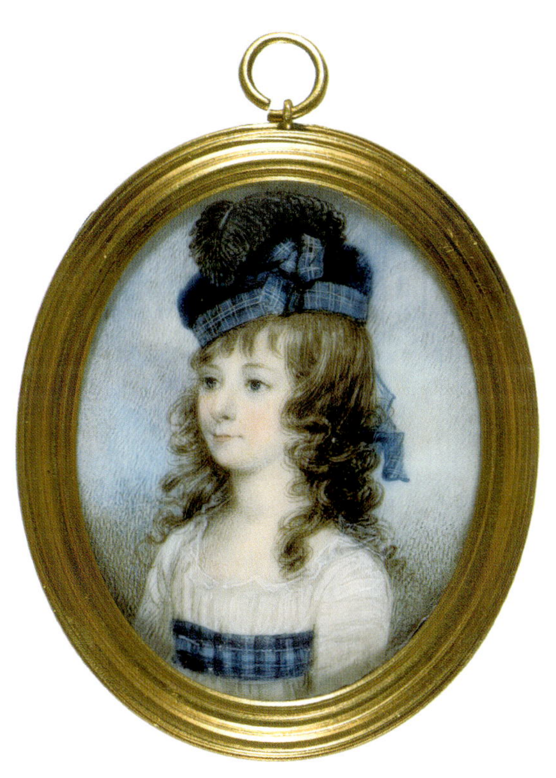

PLATE 17 · CATALOGUE 84

ANNE FOLDSONE, MRS JOSEPH MEE

Mrs Anne Murray Keith (1736–1818) c.1800–10

Watercolour on ivory, set in gilt-metal frame; 10.8 × 8cm (4¼ × 3¼in)
ENGRAVED: steel engraving by S. Freeman, *c.*1850, lettered: *S. Freeman Sc. / Mrs. Anne Murray Keith. / From a Miniatures by Mrs. Mee, in the possession / of the Countess Dowager of Hardwicke.*
COLLECTIONS: London art market in 1986
REFERENCES: *ODNB* 2004

Anne Murray Keith was the daughter of the diplomat Robert Keith of Craig, Kincardineshire, and his wife, Margaret, daughter of Sir William Cunningham of Caprington, second baronet. Her father was British minister in Vienna from 1748 to 1757, and her enamel portrait as a girl [42] was painted by Rouquet in London. The elder of her two brothers, Sir Robert Murray Keith of Murrayshall was also a diplomat and army officer [53], and in 1772 was made British envoy-extraordinary to Vienna, a post he held for twenty years. Anne Murray Keith, who despite never marrying styled herself 'Mrs' in later years, was the basis for the character Mrs Bethune Baliol in Sir Walter Scott's *Introduction to the Chronicles of Canongate*. A slightly larger version of this miniature (private collection) bears a pen and ink inscription – dated 1874 – on the verso: *Mrs Anne Murray Keith / – the Mrs Bethune Baliol of Sir / Walter Scott's Chronicles of the Canongate. / Painted by Mrs Mee.*

Anne Foldsone (*c.*1770/5–1851) was the daughter of the London-based artist and copyist John Foldsone, who died young. Foldsone was introduced to Queen Charlotte by Lady Courtown, and she was at Windsor Castle undertaking royal commissions in 1790–1. She received generous patronage from the Prince of Wales (later the Prince Regent and George IV), who commissioned her in 1812–13 to paint cabinet miniatures of the fashionable ladies of the court, known as the 'Gallery of Beauties of George III'. Foldsone married Joseph Mee, an Irishman, in 1804, and she is usually known as Mrs Mee.

PRIVATE COLLECTION

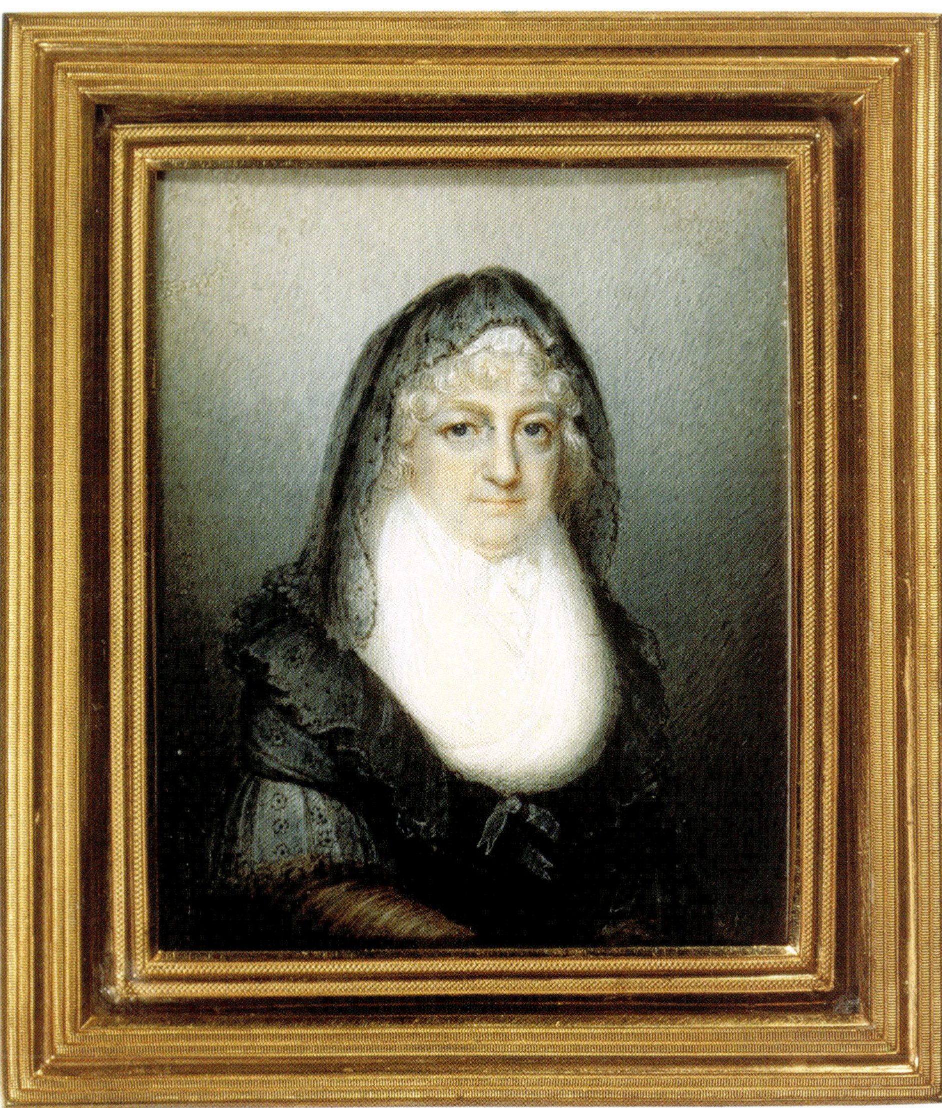

PLATE 18 · CATALOGUE 85

GEORGE SANDERS

Margaret Mercer Elphinstone, Baroness Keith and Nairn, later Comtesse de Flahault (1788–1867) 1814

Watercolour on ivory, set in gilt-metal frame; 15.2 × 10.2cm (6 × 4in); engraved on verso: *Honble. Margaret Maria Elphinstone / Countess de Flahault / 1814*
COLLECTIONS: by family descent
EXHIBITED: Edinburgh 1999, p.73, no.134

Margaret Mercer Elphinstone was the only child of the distinguished admiral Sir George Keith Elphinstone, Viscount Keith [66], and his first wife Jane Mercer, daughter and sole heiress of Colonel William Mercer. She succeeded, on the death of her father, to the two Baronies of Keith (Ireland and the United Kingdom), and on the death in 1837 of her cousin William, 4th Lord Nairn, as Baroness Nairn. When this miniature was painted she had come into contact with Lord Byron in London, who so admired her, that he presented her with his famous Albanian dress (Bowood House). She was also portrayed by Sanders in a similarly exotic Turkish dress and turban in an oil painting (private collection), which can be dated to about a year before the completion of this miniature. In 1817 the sitter married Auguste Charles Joseph, Comte de Flahault de la Billardrie (d.1870), sometime aide-de-camp to Napoleon, and later French ambassador to Vienna and London.

The Scottish artist George Sanders (1774–1846), sometimes spelt Saunders, was a significant miniaturist and oil portraitist in the Regency period. Having commenced his career in Edinburgh, he moved to London in 1805. This miniature is one of his finest works in this medium. His niece Christina Robertson was also a miniaturist, who later worked in oils at the court of the Imperial Romanov family in St Petersburg.

PRIVATE COLLECTION

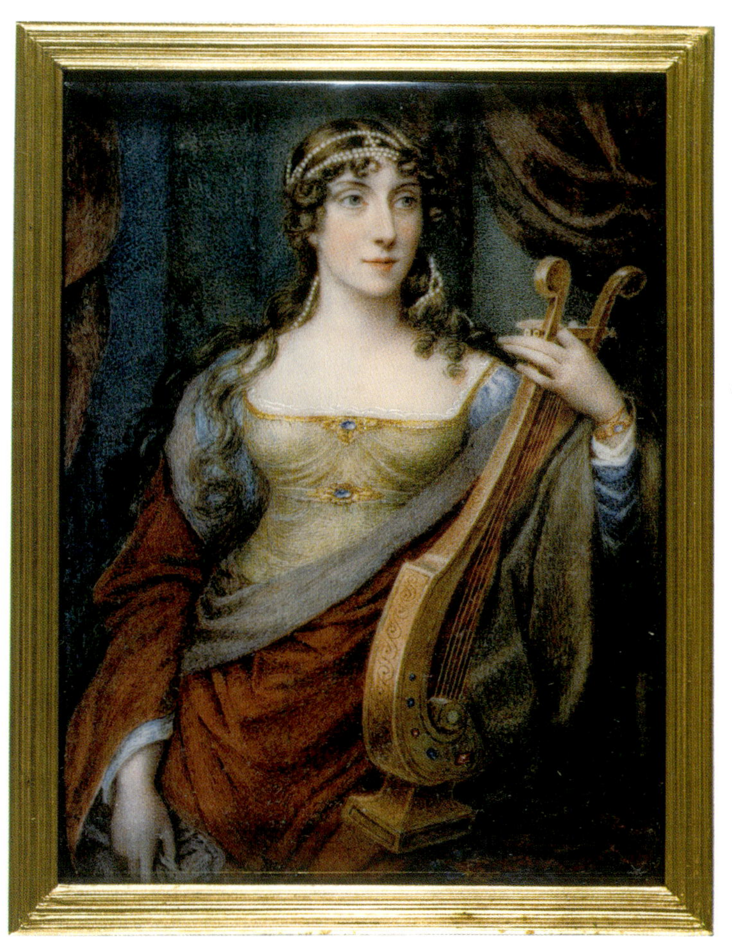

PLATE 19 · CATALOGUE 88

CHRISTINA ROBERTSON

Clementina Elizabeth Drummond-Burrell, later Baroness Aveland (1809–1888) and her sister Elizabeth Susan Drummond-Burrell, later Willoughby (1810–1853) 1819

Watercolour on ivory, set in original decorated ormolu frame, stamped with the name of the maker, *HAMLET*, the angles chiselled with scrolls, flowers and leaves in relief, enclosed in original closing leather case; 21.6 × 15.2cm (8½ × 6in); signed on recto at lower left: *CN. ROBERTSON 1819*; engraved on verso: *Clementina Elizabeth Lady Aveland / and / The Honble: Elizabeth S Drummond Willoughby / Painted in 1818 when children*

COLLECTIONS: by family descent

REFERENCES: Edinburgh 1996, p.47, ill.

EXHIBITED: London, Royal Academy, 1823, no.674 ('Portraits of the Hon. Misses Drummond Burrell'); Edinburgh 1999, p.72, no.135

The two sisters depicted – Clementina and Elizabeth – were the daughters of Peter Robert Burrell, 2nd Baron Gwydir and 19th Baron Willoughby de Eresby and his wife Clementina Sarah Drummond [73], daughter and sole heiress of the 1st and last Baron Perth and Lord Drummond of Stobhall [72]. The three-quarter length portrait miniature by George Sanders (private collection) of the mother of the two girls can be seen hanging in the background. The older sister, Clementina, in 1827 married Sir Gilbert Heathcote, 5th Bt, and later 1st Baron Aveland of Aveland. She later became Baroness Willoughby de Eresby in her own right. The younger sister, Elizabeth, died unmarried.

Born at Kinghorn in Fife, Christina Robertson (1796–1854) was the niece of the Scottish artist, George Sanders. After marrying James Robertson in 1822, she exhibited her fashionable portraits in miniature and oils of an essentially aristocratic clientele at the Royal Academy (1823–44) and at the Royal Scottish Academy (1829–45). During the 1830s she worked abroad, first in Paris in 1835–6, and later in St Petersburg, initially from 1839 to 1841. She returned there in 1847, and remained until her death, often painting full-length oil portraits.

PRIVATE COLLECTION

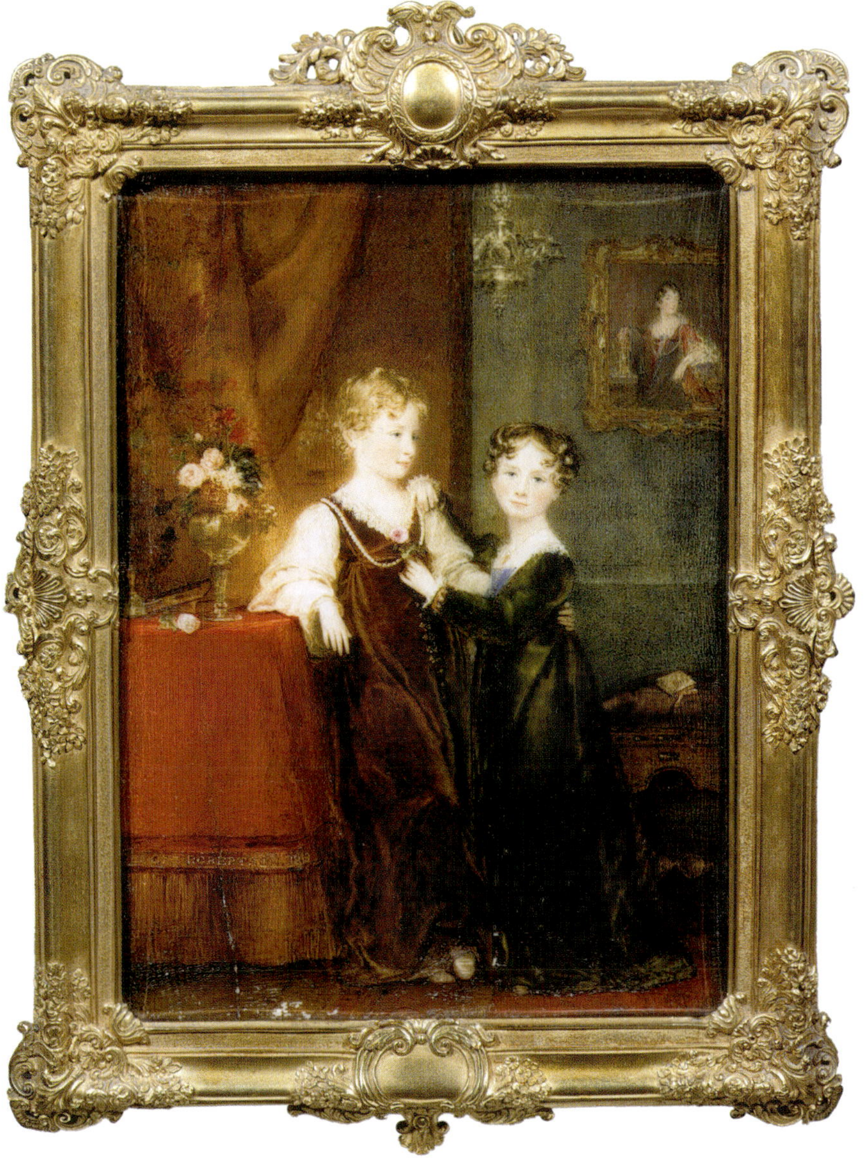

PLATE 20 · CATALOGUE 93

WILLIAM BARCLAY

Alexander William, Lord Lindsay, later 25th Earl of Crawford and 8th Earl of Balcarres (1812–1880) 1829

Watercolour on ivory, set in gilt-metal frame, set in original closing leather case; 14.1 × 10.5cm (5½ × 4¼in); signed and dated at lower left: *W Barclay / 1829*
COLLECTIONS: by family descent
REFERENCES: ODNB 2004
EXHIBITED: Edinburgh 2000, p.10, fig.1

Lord Lindsay, as he was known for much of his lifetime, was one of the nineteenth century's most significant collectors of books, manuscripts and paintings, as well as being a prolific writer on religion and art. He was the eldest son of James Lindsay, 24th Earl of Crawford and 7th Earl of Balcarres, and Maria, daughter of John Pennington, 1st Baron Muncaster. He was educated at Eton College and Trinity College, Cambridge, from where he graduated in 1833. This miniature was most probably painted to mark his leaving school and going to Cambridge, and 1829 was also the year he first travelled around Italy. Lindsay was determined not to participate in public life or stand for election to parliament, but instead acted according to his statement to a cousin in 1840: 'The cultivation of the intellect requires a private life.' Lindsay amassed a famous library – the *Bibliotheca Lindesiana* – of 30,000 volumes, choice illuminated manuscripts, and early Italian paintings, while his most important published work was *Sketches of the History of Christian Art* (1847).

Little is known about the miniaturist William Barclay (1797–1859), who was said to have been born in London. He entered the Royal Academy schools in 1819 aged twenty-two. While there has been some confusion as to his identity, he is likely to be the artist called Barclay, who exhibited at the Royal Academy from 1832 to 1856 and at the Paris Salon from 1831 to 1859.

PRIVATE COLLECTION

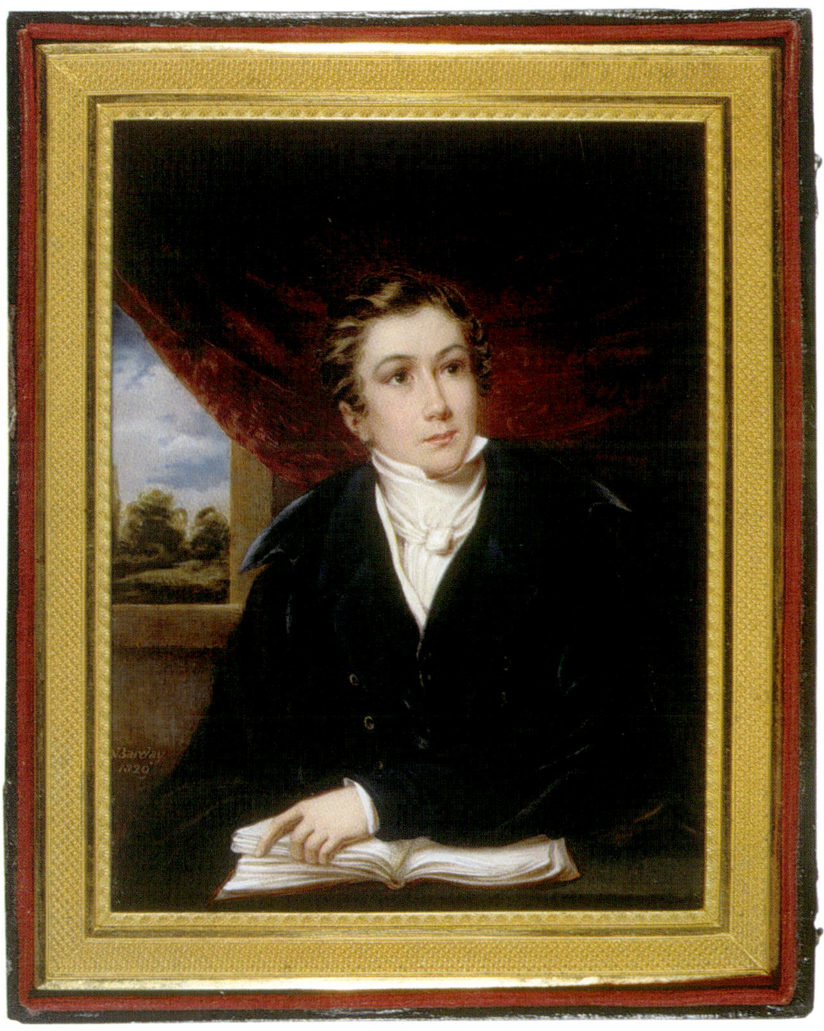
Barclay
1829

CATALOGUE

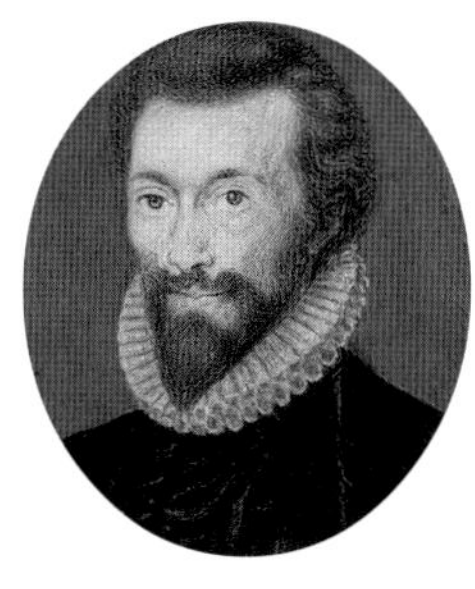

1 ISAAC OLIVER

*John Donne (1572–1631) c.*1616

Bodycolour on vellum, set in a gilt-metal frame; 4.5cm (1¾in) high
COLLECTIONS: probably acquired by Walter Francis, 5th Duke of Buccleuch; by family descent
REFERENCES: New York, San Marino, Richmond & London 1996–7, pp.94–5, no.24

John Donne was the leading metaphysical writer of the later Elizabethan and Jacobean period, and composed poetry, verse-letters, essays and sermons. Isaac Oliver (*c.*1560/5–1617) was a French limner trained in London by Nicholas Hilliard. Oliver rivalled his master in depicting the elite of English society on the small scale. The principal version of this miniature, which is signed and dated 1616, is in the Royal Collection at Windsor Castle.

IN THE COLLECTION OF THE DUKE OF BUCCLEUCH AND QUEENSBERRY KT

2 JOHN HOSKINS

*Self-portrait (c.1590–1664/5) c.*1620 [recto]; *Self-portrait drawing with five other heads* [verso]

See pages 24 and 25

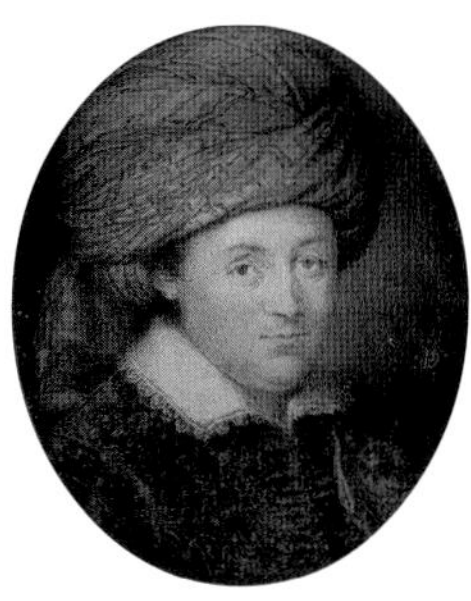

3 PETER OLIVER

*Sir Robert Shirley (c.1581–1628), 4th Bt, c.*1623–6

Bodycolour on vellum, set in gilt-metal frame; 4.6cm (1⅞in) high; signed on verso at right with monogram: *PO*; engraved on cartouche: *SIR ROBERT SHIRLEY*
COLLECTIONS: probably acquired by Walter Francis, 5th Duke of Buccleuch; by family descent
REFERENCES: McKay 1899, p.141, no.27; Kennedy 1917, pl.XII; Barnes *et al.* 2004, pp.203–5

Sir Robert Shirley was a merchant adventurer and envoy of the Shah of Persia. Famous full-length portraits of Shirley and his wife Lady Teresia, with the sitters both shown wearing Persian dress, were painted in Rome by Van Dyck during 1622, and are now at Petworth House in Sussex. This miniature was painted in London by Peter Oliver (*c.*1594–1647), the talented son of Isaac Oliver, who worked as a limner in Charles I's household.

IN THE COLLECTION OF THE DUKE OF BUCCLEUCH AND QUEENSBERRY KT

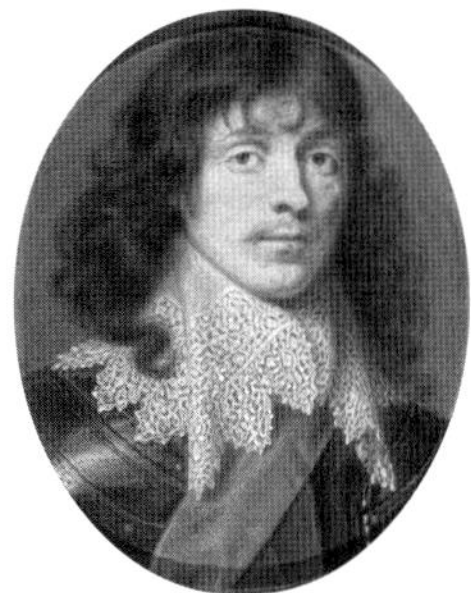

4 JOHN HOSKINS

*James Hamilton, 3rd Marquess and 1st Duke of Hamilton (1606–1649) c.*1629

Bodycolour on vellum, set in rectangular early eighteenth-century 'Lens' type ebonised wooden frame; 5.1cm (2in) high; gold lettering on recto of frame: *James, 2nd. Marquis of Hamilton.*; pen and ink inscription on verso: *James, 2nd Marquis of Hamilton / died in 1625*; number carved on verso of frame: *7*
COLLECTIONS: by descent to 4th Duke of Hamilton; his daughter Susan Douglas Hamilton; her eldest daughter Charlotte, Viscountess Hereford; her sister Susan, Lady Elcho; by family descent
REFERENCES: Smailes 1990, pp.136–9; *ODNB* 2004

The sitter was a close friend of, and principal Scottish adviser to, Charles I. This miniature is contemporary with – and closely related to – the masterly full-length of the 1st Duke painted by Daniel Mytens in 1629 (Scottish National Portrait Gallery, Edinburgh) and especially the head-

and-shoulders in armour after Mytens (Scottish National Portrait Gallery, Edinburgh). He was executed at Whitehall less than six weeks after the king. The inscriptions on this miniature are erroneous in referring to the 1st Duke's father, the 2nd Marquess, who was a significant adviser to James VI & I. Compare this portrait with two other miniatures of the sitter, when older in around 1640 [6] and 1649 [9].

THE EARL OF WEMYSS AND MARCH KT

5 JOHN HOSKINS

*Lady Mary Villiers, later Lady Herbert, and later Duchess of Lennox and Richmond (1622–1685) c.*1636

See pages 26 and 27

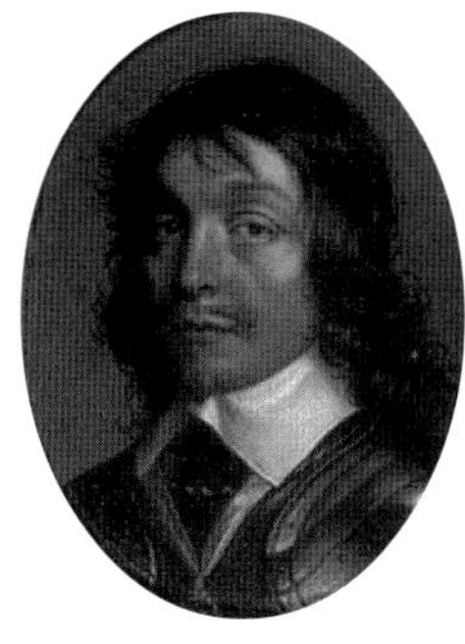

6 UNKNOWN ARTIST
AFTER SIR ANTHONY VAN DYCK

*James Hamilton, 3rd Marquess and 1st Duke of Hamilton (1606–1649) c.*1640

Oil on copper, set in closing shagreen case with crowned silver monogram on both sides; 6.6cm (2⅝in) high
COLLECTIONS: by family descent
REFERENCES: Barnes *et al.* 2004, pp.517–8, no.IV.110

This small portrait in oils was copied by an unknown artist after Van Dyck's magnificent full-length of the sitter in armour dated to 1640. This was formerly at Lennoxlove, and since 1988 has been in the collections of the Prince of Liechtenstein. Compare this oil to two other miniatures of the 1st Duke [4, 9].

IN THE COLLECTION OF LENNOXLOVE HOUSE, HADDINGTON (BY KIND PERMISSION OF THE DUKE OF HAMILTON AND BRANDON)

7 SAMUEL COOPER

*Sir Charles Compton (c.1623–1661) c.*1645–50

See pages 28 and 29

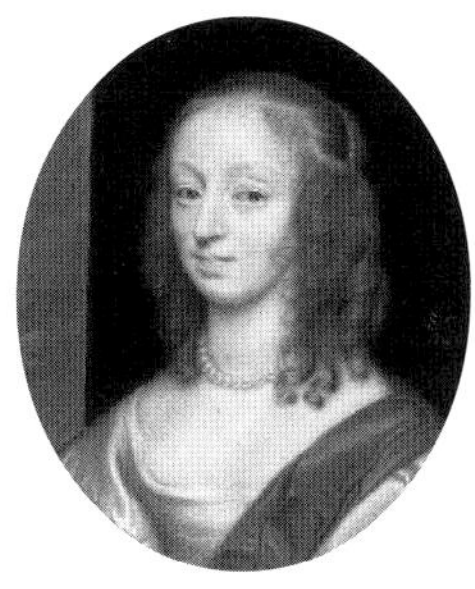

8 SAMUEL COOPER

An Unknown Lady, formerly called Mary, Princess Royal, later Princess of Orange (1631–1660) c.1647

Bodycolour on vellum, set in gilt-metal frame; 6.9cm (2¾in) high; signed in gold on recto at right: *S.C. / 1647*
COLLECTIONS: Probably acquired by Walter Francis, 5th Duke of Buccleuch; by family descent
REFERENCES: McKay 1899, p.188, no.5
EXHIBITED: London 1960–1, no.612; London 1974, no.26

This is a fine example of Cooper's work from the second half of the 1640s. It was formerly thought to represent Mary, Princess Royal, daughter of Charles I, and later Princess of Orange.

IN THE COLLECTION OF THE DUKE OF BUCCLEUCH AND QUEENSBERRY KT

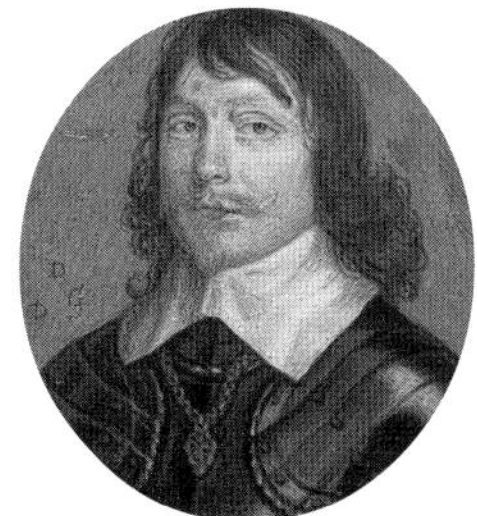

9 DAVID DES GRANGES

James Hamilton, 3rd Marquess and 1st Duke of Hamilton (1606–1649) c.1649–50

Bodycolour on vellum, set in gilt-metal frame; 3.5cm (1⅜in) high; signed on recto to left: *DDG*; engraved on verso of frame: *Duke of Hamilton*
COLLECTIONS: by family descent
REFERENCES: Edinburgh 1965, no.98

This signed miniature was probably painted after the execution of the 1st Duke, and is closely related to the larger (6.9cm high) posthumous version by Des Granges, which was signed and dated 1650 (Private Collection). Compare this miniature with two other small portraits of the sitter [4, 6]. The career of David Des Granges (*c.*1611–1671/2) began in his native London during the 1620s. In 1651 he was in Scotland for the coronation of Charles II at Scone, and was appointed the King's Limner in Scotland.

IN THE COLLECTION OF LENNOXLOVE HOUSE, HADDINGTON (BY KIND PERMISSION OF THE DUKE OF HAMILTON AND BRANDON)

10 UNKNOWN ENGLISH ARTIST

Memorial Ring with Portrait of Charles I (1600–1649) c.1649–50

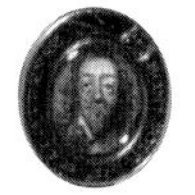

Bodycolour on vellum, set in gold ring with enamelling; 1.2cm (½in) high; portrait surrounded by enamelled Order of the Garter with motto: *HONI SOIT QUI MAL Y PENSE*; outside of ring enamelled lettering: *PRO PATRIA NON TIMIDUS MORI*
COLLECTIONS: The Dukes of Hamilton; by family descent
REFERENCES: Edinburgh 2004, p.74, no.6, ill.

This fine example is one of many such tiny portraits and rings that were made to commemorate the life and death of Charles I. For a similar example of a tiny portrait of the king, without a ring, see that on loan from the Society of Antiquaries of Scotland to the Scottish National Portrait Gallery, Edinburgh.

IN THE COLLECTION OF LENNOXLOVE HOUSE, HADDINGTON (BY KIND PERMISSION OF THE DUKE OF HAMILTON AND BRANDON)

11 NATHANIEL THACH

Sir Edward Nicholas (1593–1669) 1652

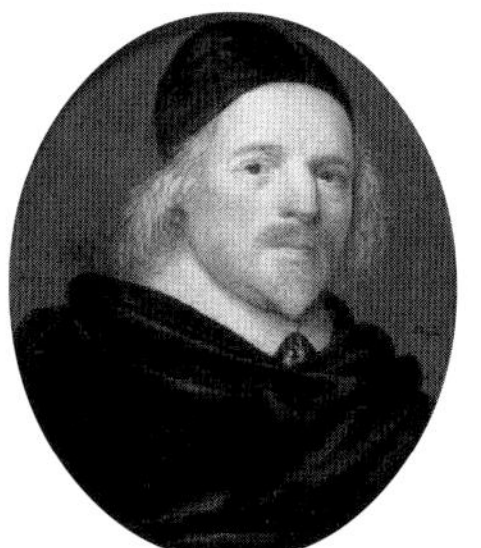

Bodycolour on vellum, set in gold locket frame enamelled in blue; 5.6cm (2¼in) high; signed at lower right: *NThach*; inscribed and dated at lower left: *AEta 59 / 1652*
COLLECTIONS: by family descent
REFERENCES: Murdoch 1997, pp.85–6; ODNB 2004

The sitter was Secretary of State to both Charles I and Charles II. Nathaniel Thach (1617– after 1652) was baptised in Barrow, Suffolk. Thach, like Alexander Cooper, may well have worked abroad at the Stuart expatriate court in The Hague. His work is scarce.

PRIVATE COLLECTION

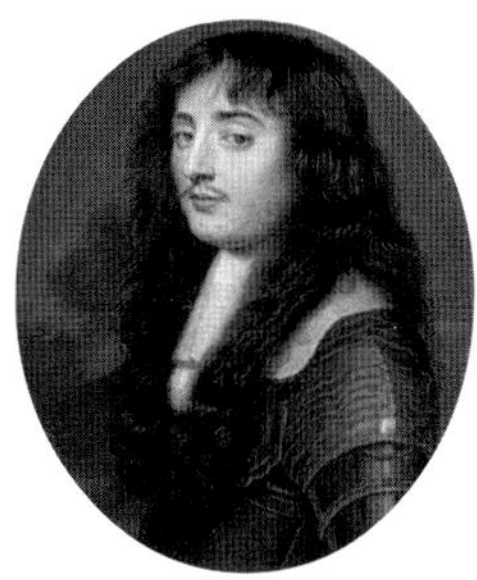

12 SAMUEL COOPER

William Douglas, Earl of Selkirk, later 3rd Duke of Hamilton (1634–1694) c.1655–6

Bodycolour on vellum, set in gilt-metal frame; 8.8cm (3⅜in) high; engraved on verso of frame: *William Earl of Selkirk / 3rd Duke of Hamilton*
COLLECTIONS: by family descent
REFERENCES: Marshall 1973, *passim*

William, Earl of Selkirk, was the eldest son of William, 1st Marquess of Douglas. In 1656 he married Anne, Duchess of Hamilton in her own right, and he became 3rd Duke of Hamilton for life. This miniature, which is a good example of Cooper's style from the mid-1650s, may have been painted to mark his engagement or marriage.

IN THE COLLECTION OF LENNOXLOVE HOUSE, HADDINGTON (BY KIND PERMISSION OF THE DUKE OF HAMILTON AND BRANDON)

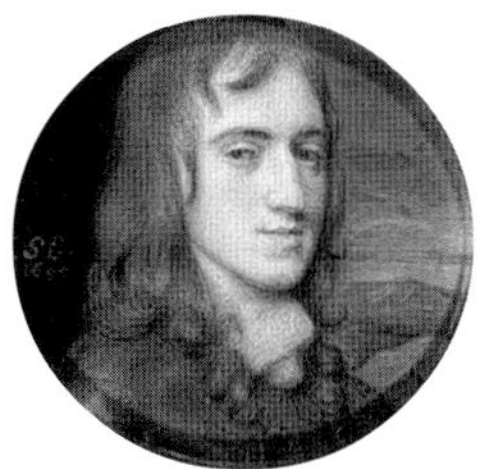

13 SAMUEL COOPER

An Unknown Gentleman, formerly called Charles Stuart, 6th Duke of Lennox and 3rd Duke of Richmond (1640–1672) 1655

Bodycolour on vellum, set in mid-nineteenth-century gold filigree frame; 1.8cm (¾in) dia.; signed with initials and dated at left: *S.C. / 1655*; engraved on verso of frame: *Charles Stuart / Duke of Lennox / and Richmond / by S. Cooper*
COLLECTIONS: Probably acquired by Walter Francis, 5th Duke of Buccleuch; by family descent
REFERENCES: McKay 1899, p.142, no.31; Williamson 1906–8, I, pp.105–6, no.123, pl.LV(1); *ODNB* 2004

This portrait is the smallest of Cooper's miniatures and shows astonishing virtuosity by the artist. An almost identical miniature signed and dated 1658, formerly in the collection of J. Pierpont Morgan, was identified by George Williamson as being Richard Cromwell, son of the Lord Protector, although that version was likely to be a copy of this work. Charles Stuart, 6th Duke of Lennox and 3rd Duke of Richmond, was the only son of George Stuart, 9th seigneur d'Aubigny, who was fourth son of Esmé, 3rd Duke of Lennox.

IN THE COLLECTION OF THE DUKE OF BUCCLEUCH AND QUEENSBERRY KT

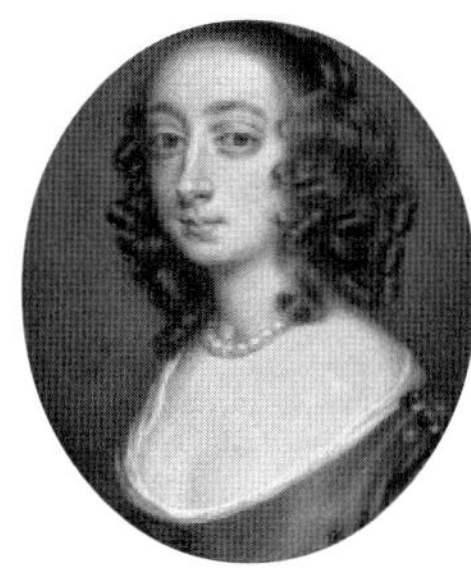

14 RICHARD GIBSON

*Elizabeth Percy, Countess of Essex (1636–1718) c.*1655–60

Bodycolour on vellum, set in scroll-topped metal frame;
5.6cm (2¼in) high
COLLECTIONS: Mrs Daphne Foskett
REFERENCES: Foskett 1979, pl.24c; Edinburgh 1996–7, p.89, no.54
EXHIBITED: London 1974, p.106, no.203, ill.

A smaller version of this miniature is at Castle Howard. Elizabeth Percy also appears in Gibson's double portrait miniature with her husband Arthur, 1st Earl of Essex, in the Buccleuch collection. She was the daughter of Algernon Percy, 10th Earl of Northumberland, and was married in 1653. Her husband, having been committed to the Tower, was later found there with his throat cut.

PRIVATE COLLECTION

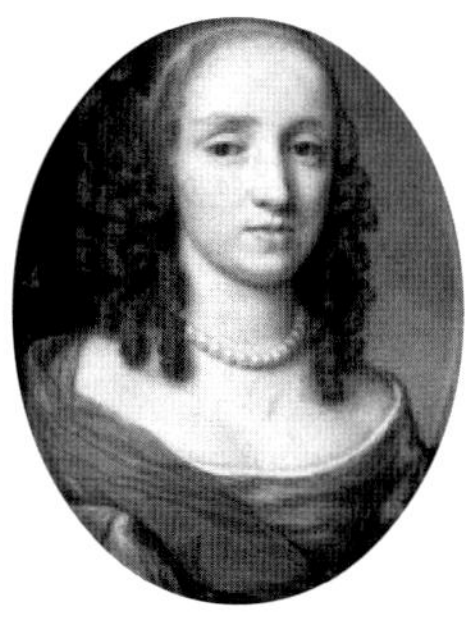

15 SAMUEL COOPER

*An Unknown Lady, formerly called Mary, Princess Royal, later Princess of Orange (1631–1660) c.*1655–60

Bodycolour on vellum, set in gilt-metal frame; 6.9cm (2¾in) high; signed with monogram on recto to left: *SC*
COLLECTIONS: Probably acquired by Walter Francis, 5th Duke of Buccleuch; by family descent
REFERENCES: McKay 1899, p.187, no.4
EXHIBITED: London 1889, p.6, no.23; London 1916–20, pl.19; London 1974, p.16, no.28, ill.

The sitter in this miniature by Cooper was formerly thought to by Mary, Princess Royal, daughter of Charles I, and later Princess of Orange.

IN THE COLLECTION OF THE DUKE OF BUCCLEUCH AND QUEENSBERRY KT

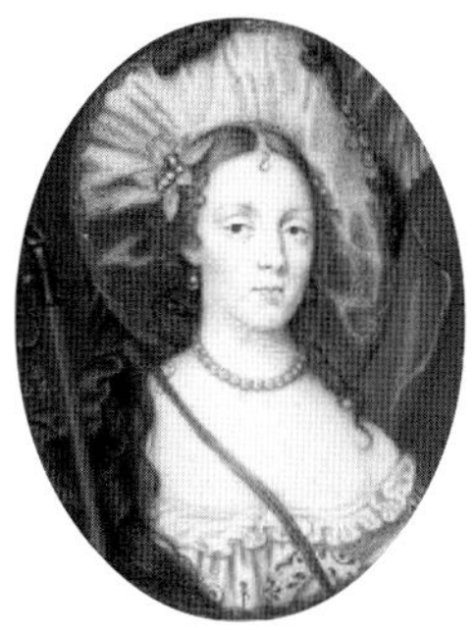

16 DAVID DES GRANGES AFTER JACOB HUYSMANS

Catherine of Braganza (1638–1705) c.1664–5

Bodycolour on vellum, set in scroll-topped gilt-metal frame; 8.2cm (3¼in) high; signed in gold lettering on recto to left: *DDG*
COLLECTIONS: Greta S. Heckett collection; her sale, Sotheby's, London, 11 July 1977, lot 155; Mrs Daphne Foskett
REFERENCES: London and New Haven 2001–2, p.59

This miniature is a partial and adapted copy by Des Granges after the full-length oil of Charles II's consort as a shepherdess by Jacob Huysmans, dated 1664, and now in the Royal Collection at Windsor Castle.

PRIVATE COLLECTION

17 RICHARD GIBSON AFTER SIR PETER LELY

Elizabeth Wriothesley, Lady Percy, later Countess of Northumberland (1645/6–1690) c.1665–70

See pages 30 and 31

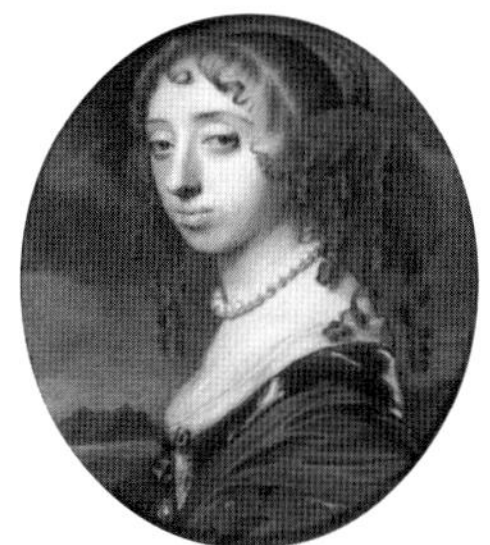

18 SAMUEL COOPER

Lady Amelia Ann Sophia Stanley, Marchioness of Atholl (d.1703) 1667

Bodycolour on vellum, set in gold locket frame; 7.6cm (3in) high; signed with monogram and dated on recto: *SC / 1667*; inscribed in pen and ink on paper on verso: *Lady Amelia Stanley / wife of / John, 1st Marquis of Atholl*
COLLECTIONS: by family descent
EXHIBITED: London 1974, p.55, no.121, ill.
See illustration on front cover

The sitter was the fourth daughter and sole heiress of James, 7th Earl of Derby, KG. In 1659 she married John Murray, 2nd Earl and 1st Marquess of Atholl, who through her inherited the sovereignty of the Isle of Man. This miniature by Cooper is in especially good condition and the red pigments in the sitter's dress have notably retained their brilliance.

BLAIR CHARITABLE TRUST (FROM THE COLLECTION OF BLAIR CASTLE, BLAIR ATHOLL)

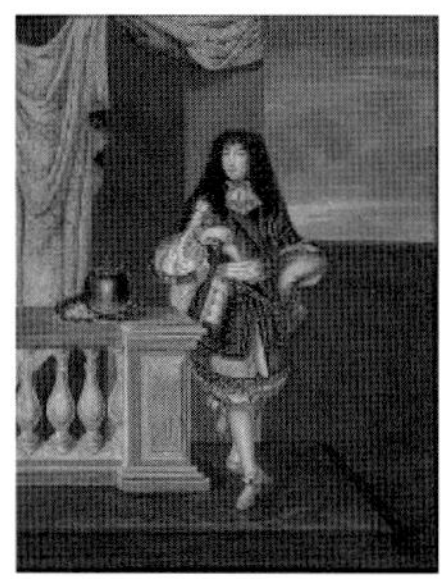

19 UNKNOWN FRENCH ARTIST

Philippe, duc d'Orléans (1640–1701) c.1670–5

Bodycolour on vellum, set in nineteenth-century gilt-metal frame; 17.1 × 12.1cm (6¾ × 4¾in); engraved on cartouche: *PHILIPPE DUC D'ORLEANS*
COLLECTIONS: Probably acquired by Walter Francis, 5th Duke of Buccleuch; by family descent
REFERENCES: McKay 1899, p.65, no.10
The sitter was the younger brother of Louis XIV.

IN THE COLLECTION OF THE DUKE OF BUCCLEUCH AND QUEENSBERRY KT

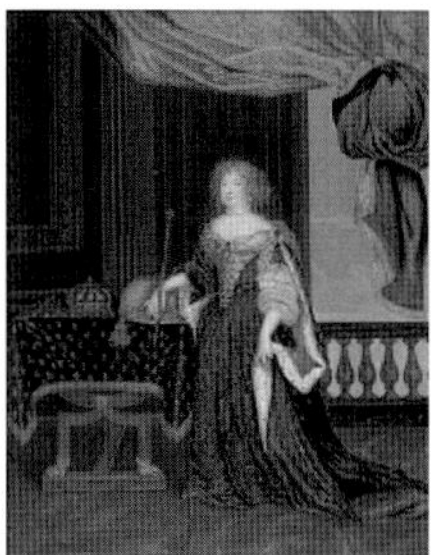

20 UNKNOWN FRENCH ARTIST

Maria Theresa of Spain (1638–1683) c.1670–5

Bodycolour on vellum, set in nineteenth-century gilt-metal frame; 17.1 × 12.1cm (6¾ × 4in); cartouche engraved: ANNE D'AUTRICHE
COLLECTIONS: Probably acquired by Walter Francis, 5th Duke of Buccleuch; by family descent
REFERENCES: McKay 1899, p.66, no.16

The Infanta Maria Theresa, daughter of Philip IV of Spain, married Louis XIV in 1660 as his first wife. The sitter in this miniature was formerly identified as Ann of Austria, Queen of Louis XIII.

IN THE COLLECTION OF THE DUKE OF BUCCLEUCH AND QUEENSBERRY KT

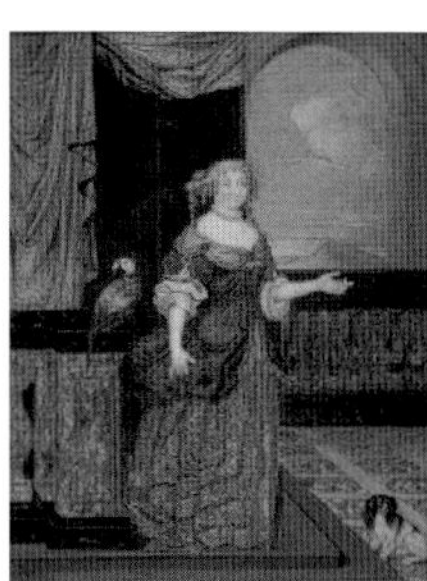

21 UNKNOWN FRENCH ARTIST

Marquise de Montespan (1641–1707) c.1670–5

Bodycolour on vellum, set in nineteenth-century gilt-metal frame; 17.1 × 12.1cm (6¾ × 4in); cartouche engraved: *MADAME DE MONTESPAU* [sic]
COLLECTIONS: Probably acquired by Walter Francis, 5th Duke of Buccleuch; by family descent
REFERENCES: McKay 1899, p.55, no.12

Françoise Athénais de Rochechouart, Madame de Montespan, was daughter of the duc de Mortemar, and a mistress of Louis XIV.

IN THE COLLECTION THE DUKE OF BUCCLEUCH AND QUEENSBERRY KT

22 DAVID LOGGAN

Edward Nicholas (b.1624 – after 1672) 1672

See pages 32 and 33

23 W.P. (POSSIBLY WILLIAM PAWLETT)

*Mary Davis (fl.1660 – after 1698) c.*1673

See pages 34 and 35

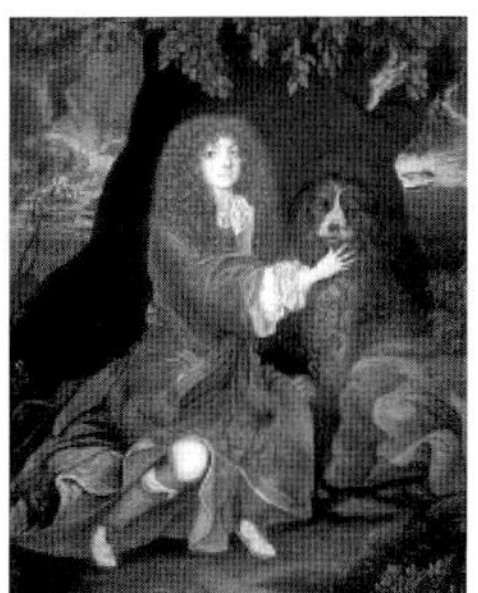

24 D.M. (POSSIBLY D. MYERS)

Henry Fitzroy. 1st Duke of Grafton (1663–1690) 1675–6

Bodycolour on vellum; 20.3 × 15.2cm (8 × 6in); signed with gold monogram and dated: *DM / 1675/6*
COLLECTIONS: Probably acquired by Walter Francis, 5th Duke of Buccleuch; by family descent
REFERENCES: McKay 1899, p.184, no.6; Kennedy 1917, pl.XLV; Murdoch 1997, p.293

The sitter was the natural son of Charles II and his mistress Barbara Villiers, Countess of Castlemaine and later Duchess of Cleveland. Although a number of miniatures from the 1660s and 1670s have survived with the monogrammed signature *DM*, the exact identity of this talented amateur artist remains elusive. The name D. Myers has been suggested tentatively.

IN THE COLLECTION OF THE DUKE OF BUCCLEUCH AND QUEENSBERRY KT

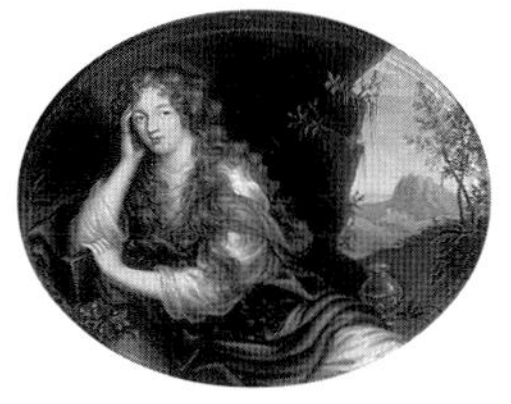

25 AN UNKNOWN ARTIST AFTER HENRI GASCAR

*Françoise, duchesse de La Vallière (1664–1710) c.*1675–80

Bodycolour on vellum, set in eighteenth-century gilt-metal frame; 12.1cm (4¾in) high; engraved on cartouche: *MADLLE LA VALLIERE.*
COLLECTIONS: Probably acquired by Walter Francis, 5th Duke of Buccleuch; by family descent
REFERENCES: McKay 1899, p.51, no.5

Françoise Louise de la Baume le Blanc, duchesse de La Vallière, was the mistress of Louis XIV, before being supplanted by Madame de Montespan. Henri Gascar (*c.*1635–1701) was French portraitist who worked for a while at the court of Charles II in England.

IN THE COLLECTION OF THE DUKE OF BUCCLEUCH AND QUEENSBERRY KT

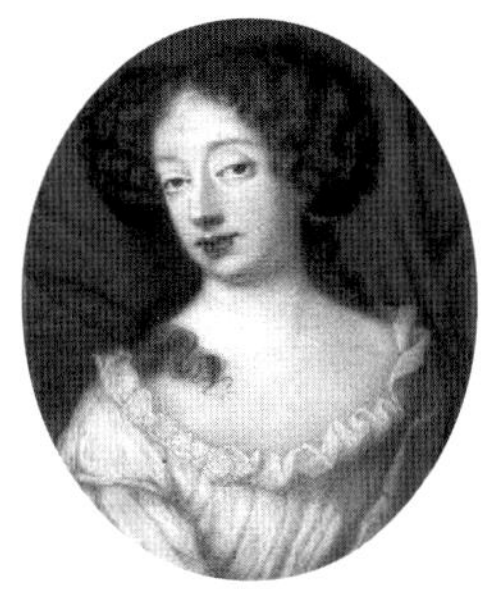

26 NICHOLAS DIXON AFTER SIR PETER LELY

*Mary of Modena (1658–1718) c.*1675

Bodycolour on vellum, set in late nineteenth-century decorated gilt-metal frame; 8.5cm (3⅜ins) high; engraved on verso of frame: *Mistress Nell Gwynne / by / Samuel Cooper*; inscribed in pen and ink on verso of frame: *280*
COLLECTIONS: Greta S. Heckett; her sale (part IV) at Sotheby's, London, 24 April 1978, lot 509; Mrs Daphne Foskett
REFERENCES: Foskett 1979, pl.27G; London & New Haven 2001–2, pp.158–9
EXHIBITED: London 1993, p.45, col. pl.

Mary of Modena was the second wife and consort of James VII & II. Nicholas Dixon (*c.*1645 – after 1708) succeeded Samuel Cooper as limner to Charles II and keeper of the king's picture closet, receiving an annuity of £200 per annum. This miniature is a partial and adapted copy after the oil by Lely belonging to the Earl Spencer at Althorp Park.

PRIVATE COLLECTION

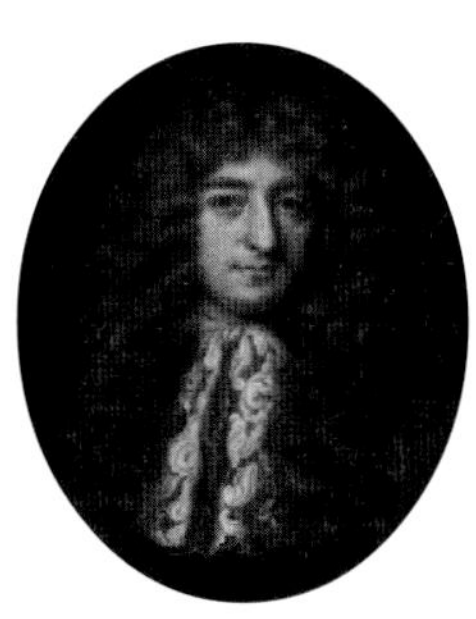

27 PETER CROSS

*James Drummond, 4th Earl and 1st titular Duke of Perth (1648–1716) c.*1685–8

Bodycolour on vellum, set in gilt-metal frame, 8.8cm (3⅛in) high; signed on recto with monogram: *PC*; engraved of verso of frame: *E. of Perth / Ld. Chancellor*
COLLECTIONS: by family descent
REFERENCES: Jamieson 1993, p.4, col. pl.

The sitter was appointed to the Privy Council in 1678, became Justice General in 1882 and was made Lord High Chancellor of Scotland in 1684. A supporter of James VII & II he went into exile in France in 1692, where both he and his brother, the Earl of Melfort, were created Jacobite dukes.

PRIVATE COLLECTION

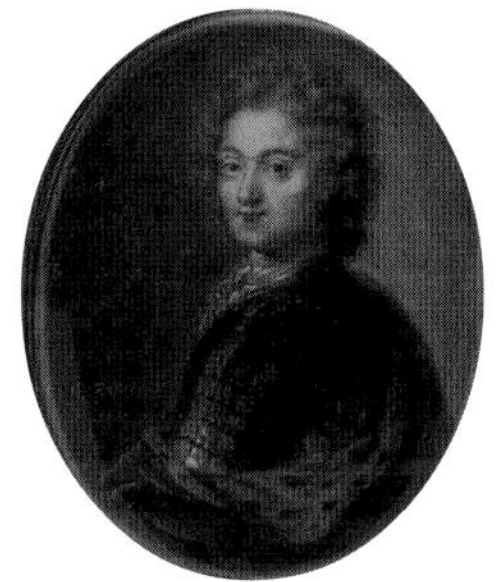

28 C. TASSIS AFTER FRANCOIS DE TROY

James Drummond, known as the Marquis of Drummond, later 5th Earl and 2nd titular Duke of Perth (1674–1720) 1694

Bodycolour on card, set in gilt-metal frame; 6.3cm (2½in) high; signed and dated on recto: *C. Tassis F / 1694*; engraved on verso of frame: *Marq. Of Drummond*
COLLECTIONS: by family descent
REFERENCES: Jamieson 1993
EXHIBITED: St Germain 1992, p.241, ill.

The sitter, who was the son of the 4th Earl and 1st titular Duke of Perth, spent much of his early adulthood in France, but joined the Earl of Mar in 1715 Jacobite Rising. Very little is known of the French miniaturist Tassis. This miniature is a faithful copy of an oil portrait of the sitter (Private Collection) painted in 1694 by François de Troy, one of the leading painters at the French court. The sitter was portrayed as an older man in a miniature by Benjamin Arlaud [31].

PRIVATE COLLECTION

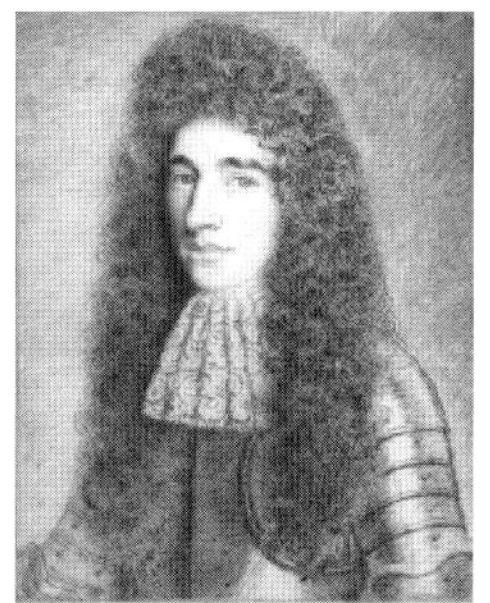

29 DAVID PATON

Charles Stuart, 4th Earl of Traquair (1659–1741) 1694

Plumbago (lead point) on vellum, set in gilt-wood and ebonised wooden frame; 12 × 9.5cm (4¾ × 3¾in)
COLLECTIONS: by family descent

The sitter was a Jacobite who was involved in the 1715 Rising. This portrait – together with the untraced paired plumbago of his wife – was made to mark his marriage in 1694 to Mary Maxwell, only daughter of Robert Maxwell, 4th Earl of Nithsdale. David Paton (fl.1665 – after 1709) was the outstanding Scottish portrait draughtsman and copyist of his generation. Much of his work survives at Ham House in Richmond near London, the home of his most important patrons, the Duke of Lauderdale and his wife Elizabeth Murray, Countess of Dysart.

TRAQUAIR HOUSE CHARITABLE TRUST

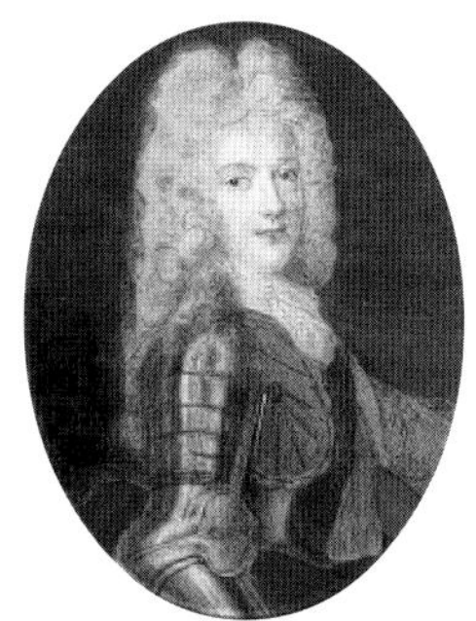

30 JACQUELINE DE LA BOISSIERE

Prince James Francis Edward Stuart (1688–1766) c.1710

Bodycolour on vellum, set in eighteenth-century scroll-topped gold locket frame; 8.9cm (3½in) high; engraved on nineteenth-century cartouche at top: *PRINCE JAMES FRANCIS EDWARD STUART / PRINCE OF WALES. / CHEVALIER OF ST. GEORGE / BORN 1688. DIED 1766. / GIVEN BY H.R.H. TO SIR WM. STIRLING / 4TH. BARONET OF ARDOCH.*; back of gold locket engraved and chased with royal coat of arms surrounded by the Garter, engraved: *HONI SOIT [QUI] MAL Y PENSE*; and surmounted with pennant engraved: *NEMO ME IMPUNE LACESSIT*

COLLECTIONS: given by the sitter to Sir William Stirling, 4th Baronet of Ardoch; by family descent

REFERENCES: Edinburgh 2001A, pp.46–7, col. pl. and p.107

The sitter (the Old Pretender) was the son of James VII & II and his second wife Mary of Modena. His birth precipitated the Glorious Revolution of 1688, and he spent the rest of his life in exile in France and Italy. Jacqueline de La Boissière was one of a group of French miniaturists – including Jacques-Antoine Arlaud and Anne Chéron – who were employed by the Jacobites at the court in St Germain to make miniature copies of their portraits for distibution as diplomatic gifts and tokens of loyalty.

PRIVATE COLLECTION

31 BENJAMIN ARLAUD

James Drummond, known as the Marquis of Drummond, later 5th Earl and 2nd titular Duke of Perth (1674–1720) c.1710–15

Bodycolour on vellum, set in gilt-metal frame; 7cm (2¾in) high;

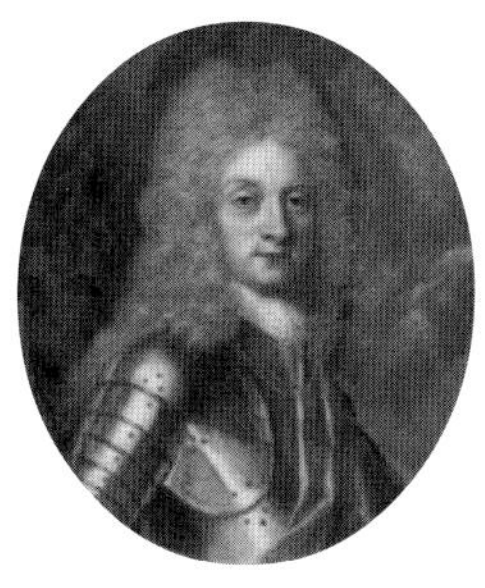

engraved on verso: *J.D.* with *M* under a coronet
COLLECTIONS: by family descent

The sitter was portrayed in a miniature by Tassis as a younger man [28]. Benjamin Arlaud (*c.*1670–1719?) was a Swiss-born miniaturist active in London from around 1704 to 1717.

PRIVATE COLLECTION

32 BERNARD LENS III AFTER SIR GODFREY KNELLER
*James Douglas, Earl of Arran, later 4th Duke of Hamilton (1658–1712) c.*1712

See pages 36 and 37

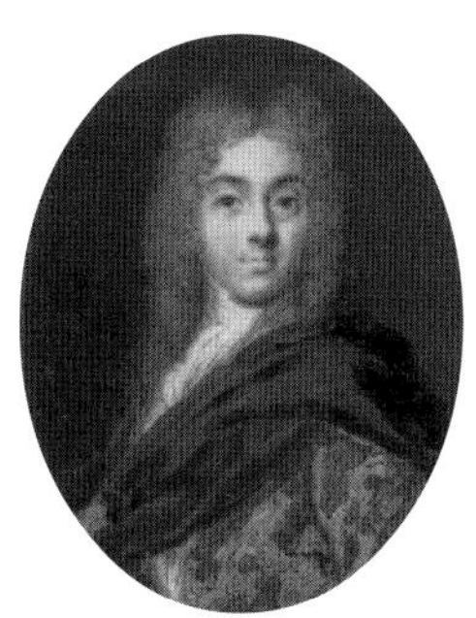

33 ROSALBA CARRIERA
*An Unknown Nobleman, possibly William Murray, 2nd Marquis of Tullibardine (1689–1746) c.*1720

Watercolour on ivory, set in gilt-metal frame; 8.3cm (3¼in) high; engraved on verso of frame: *P. Chas. Edward.*
COLLECTIONS: by family descent

The sitter has traditionally been identified as Prince Charles Edward Stuart, although this portrait does not look like any other known portraits of the Young Pretender. A more likely candidate is the Jacobite, William Murray, 2nd Marquis of Tullibardine, who was the second son of John Murray, 1st Duke of Atholl. His miniature by Rosalba, painted at this date, and showing him wearing a different more patterned dress, is at Blair Castle. The Venetian woman artist Rosalba Carriera (1675–1757) was one of the most fashionable portraitists working in Italy and France during the first half of the eighteenth century. She was highly esteemed for her Rococo pastels, and also pioneered the technique of painting miniatures on ivory.

PRIVATE COLLECTION

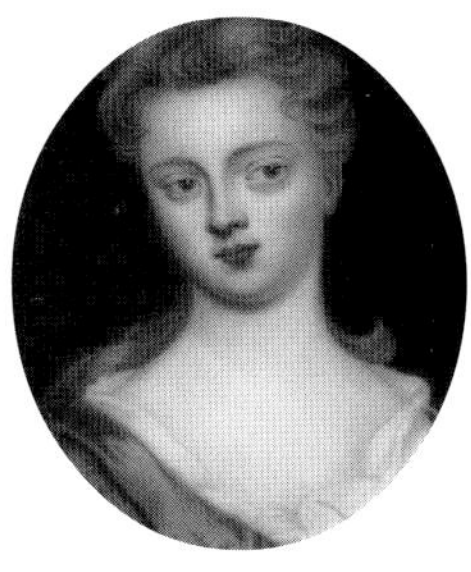

34 CHARLES BOIT

Rachel Guise, Lady Bradshaigh (1701–1743) c.1720

Enamel on copper, set in gilt-metal frame; 3.7cm (1½in) high; signed on counter enamel: *C Boit f*; inscribed in eighteenth-century hand in pen and ink on accompanying piece of paper: *Rachel d / of Sir John / Guise, married / to Sir Rogr / Bradshaw* [sic]
COLLECTIONS: by family descent
REFERENCES: Coffin & Hofstetter 2000, p.100, no.49

The sitter was the daughter of Sir John Guise and married Sir Roger Bradshaigh, Bt, of Haigh. Charles Boit (1662–1727) was born in Stockholm and was the leading enamellist in London from 1696, though he also spent time in Dresden before settling in Paris, where he died.

PRIVATE COLLECTION

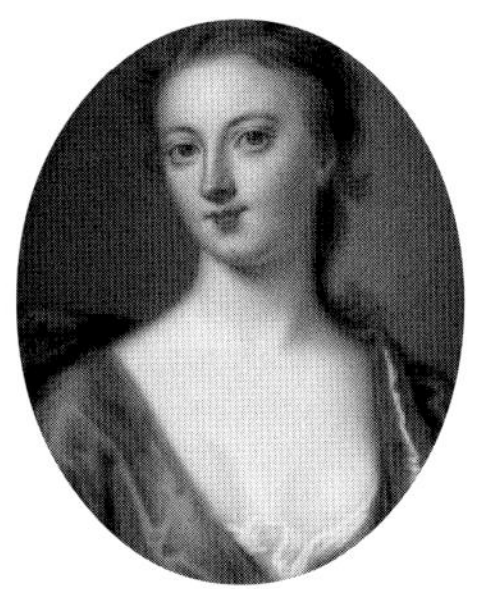

35 CHRISTIAN FRIEDRICH ZINCKE

An Unknown Lady, possibly Elizabeth Strangways, Duchess of Hamilton (d.1729) c.1727

Enamel on copper, set in gilt-metal frame; 4.1cm (1⅝in) high; engraved on verso of frame: *Lady Anne Spencer / Wife of the / 4th. Duke of Hamilton*
COLLECTIONS: by family descent

The inscription on the back of this miniature cannot be correct, as the portrait is too late to be Anne Spencer, the first wife of James, 4th Duke of Hamilton. It is more likely to be a portrait of the 5th Duke of Hamilton's second wife, Elizabeth, daughter of Thomas Strangways, who was married in 1727. The sitter resembles an oil portrait of Elizabeth Strangways by William Aikman at Lennoxlove. The Dresden-born portraitist Christian Friedrich Zincke (1683/4–1767) was the leading enameller in London, after the death of his master, the Swede Charles Boit.

IN THE COLLECTION OF LENNOXLOVE HOUSE, HADDINGTON (BY KIND PERMISSION OF THE DUKE OF HAMILTON AND BRANDON)

36 WILLIAM PREWETT
Horatio (or Horace) Walpole, 4th Earl of Orford (1717–1797) 1735

See pages 38 and 39

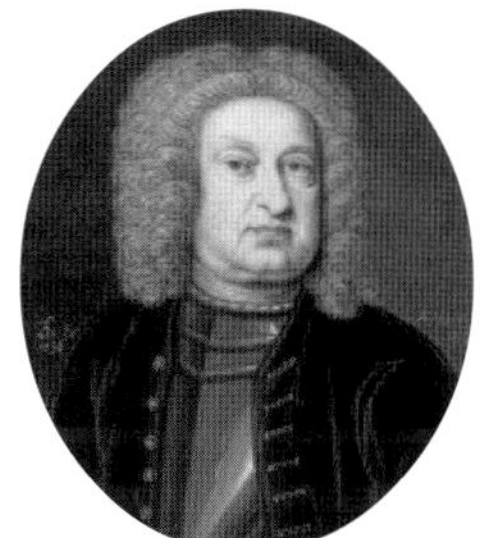

37 BERNARD LENS III
General Hatton Compton (1656 – after 1736) 1736

Watercolour on ivory; set in metal frame; 8cm (3⅛in) high; inscribed, signed with monogram and dated in gold on recto: *BL. Fe. / 1737 / AEtatis. / 80.* scratched on verso of frame: *General Compton / Grand-father to Lady Muncaster*
COLLECTIONS: by family descent
REFERENCES: Coffin & Hofstetter 2000, p.100, col. pl.

The sitter, who was deputy lieutenant of the Tower of London, was a member of the Compton family and closely related to the Marquesses of Northampton. In 1685 he inherited Grendon Hall in Northamptonshire. In 1713 the general inherited the important tenth-century illuminated manuscript, known as *The Benedictional of St Aethelwold* from his uncle, Henry Compton, Bishop of London. He gave this manuscript to William Cavendish, 2nd Duke of Devonshire, from whose descendants it was purchased by the British Library, London. This miniature by Lens, which is in excellent condition, was copied in an enamel, attributed to Noah Seaman (fl.1724–*c*.1741), now in the Gilbert Collection, London.

PRIVATE COLLECTION

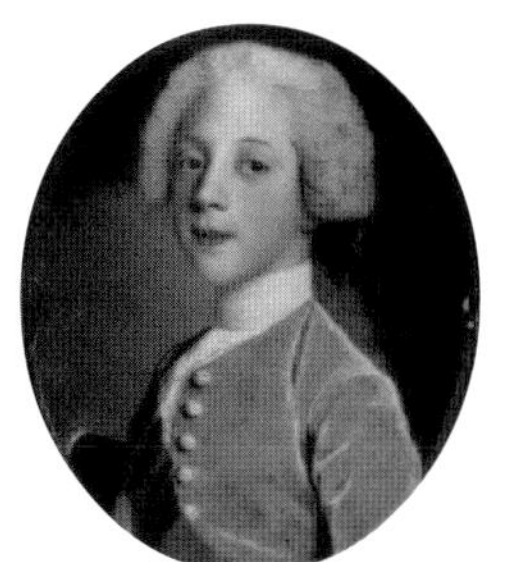

38 JEAN-ETIENNE LIOTARD
*Prince Henry Benedict Stuart (1725–1807) c.*1736

Enamel on copper, set in gilt-metal frame; 5.4cm (2⅛in) high; engraved on verso of frame: *P. Chas.*
COLLECTIONS: by family descent
EXHIBITED: London 1993, no.78, col. pl.

The sitter was the second son of Prince James Francis Edward Stuart and Princess Maria Clementina Sobieska, and the younger brother of Prince

Charles Edward Stuart. He was made Cardinal York in 1747. Jean-Etienne Liotard (1702–1789), who was the leading itinerant pastellist in Europe and the Ottoman Empire during the mid-eighteenth century, painted the Stuart brothers in Rome in 1736, and a number of variants were made. This was formerly and erroneously known as a portrait of Prince Charles Edward Stuart.

PRIVATE COLLECTION

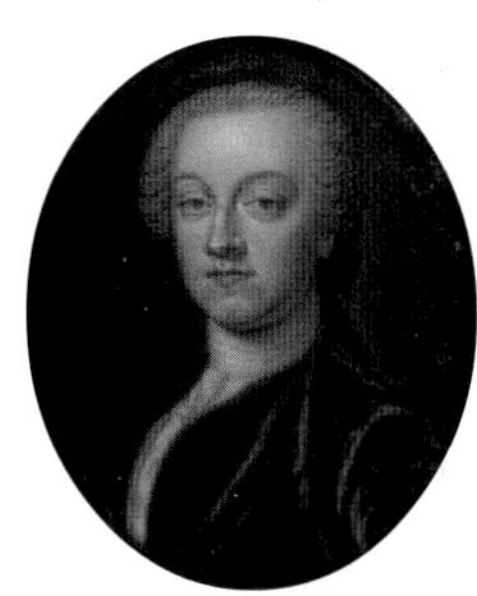

39 UNKNOWN ENGLISH ARTIST

Anthony Tracy-Keck (1712–1767) c.1736

Enamel on copper, set in ornamental gold frame decorated with enamelled flowers, verso enclosing a glazed compartment with sitters hair; 5.1cm (2in) high
COLLECTIONS: by family descent

Anthony Tracy-Keck of Great Tew in Oxfordshire married Lady Susan Douglas-Hamilton [40], daughter of James, 4th Duke of Hamilton [32] and his second wife Elizabeth Gerard in 1736. In 1754 he was elected Member of Parliament for the pocket borough of New Woodstock. This enamel is by the same artist as painted the portrait of an unknown gentleman now in the Gilbert Collection, London (see Coffin & Hofstetter 2000, pp.98–9, no.47). That miniature is attributed to Jean-André Rouquet although it is very unlike his style of painting. This is likely to be a marriage portrait, no doubt intended to be given to the sitter's wife.

THE EARL OF WEMYSS AND MARCH KT

40 CHRISTIAN FRIEDRICH ZINCKE

Lady Susan Douglas-Hamilton, Mrs Anthony Tracy-Keck (d.1755) c.1736

Enamel on copper, set in gold frame with verso engraved with sitter's coat-of-arms; 5.1cm (2in) high
COLLECTIONS: by family descent

The sitter, who was daughter of James, 4th Duke of Hamilton [32] married Anthony Tracy-Keck [39] of Great Tew in Oxfordshire in 1736.

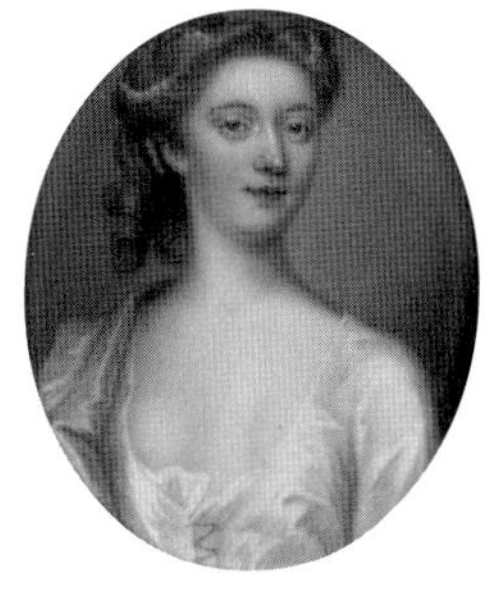

The lavish back of this gold locket, which is engraved with the sitters' coat of arms, indicates that this enamel was very likely to have been a marriage portrait, to be given to her husband.

THE EARL OF WEMYSS AND MARCH KT

41 JEAN-ANDRE ROUQUET

James Drummond, 6th Earl and 3rd titular Duke of Perth (1713–1746) c.1740

See pages 40 and 41

42 JEAN-ETIENNE LIOTARD

Maria Theresa, Empress of Austria (1717–1780) 1743

inside smaller lid

JEAN-ETIENNE LIOTARD

Duchess Maria Anna (1718–1744) 1744

inside larger lid

JEAN-ANDRE ROUQUET

Miss Anne Murray Keith (1736–1818) c.1745

opposite smaller lid

See pages 42 and 43

43 JOHN DANIEL KAMM
AFTER MAURICE-QUENTIN DE LA TOUR

Prince Charles Edward Stuart (1720–1788) c.1749–50

See pages 44 and 45

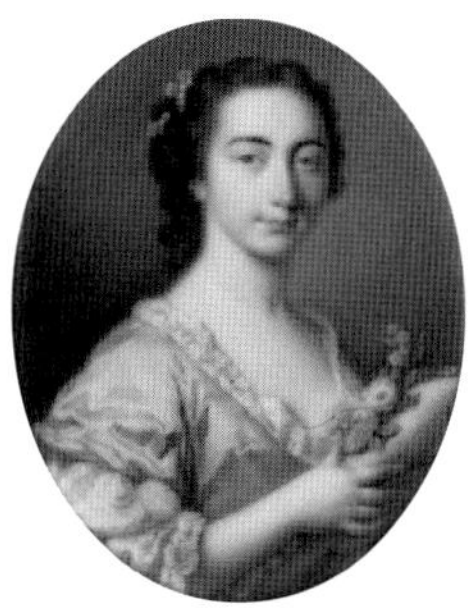

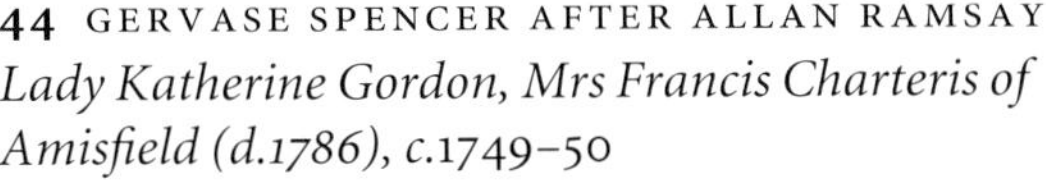

44 GERVASE SPENCER AFTER ALLAN RAMSAY

*Lady Katherine Gordon, Mrs Francis Charteris of Amisfield (d.1786), c.*1749–50

Enamel on copper, set onto lid of gold and enamelled oval snuff-box by Jean-Joseph Barrière, made between 1775 and 1781, with original shagreen box; 5.5cm (2½in) high
COLLECTIONS: by family descent
EXHIBITED: Edinburgh 1999, p.56, no.17

Lady Katherine Gordon, the sixth daughter of Alexander, 2nd Duke of Gordon, married Francis Charteris of Amisfield in 1745. Charteris became 7th Earl of Wemyss [59] in 1787. This enamel was copied from a full-length portrait of the couple painted by Allan Ramsay in around 1750 and now at Gosford House. Gervase Spencer (*c.*1715–1763) was a fashionable portrait miniaturist working in London during the 1750s and early 1760s in both watercolour on ivory and enamel.

THE EARL OF WEMYSS AND MARCH KT

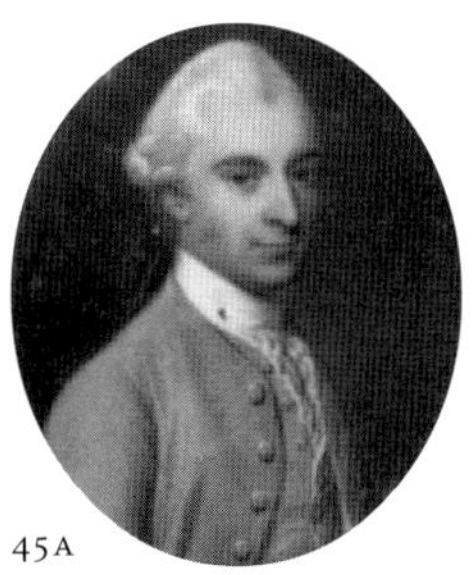

45A

45 VARIOUS ARTISTS

A Frame of Ten Portrait Miniatures

COLLECTIONS: by family descent
REFERENCES: Maxwell Stuart 1986, p.27, ill.

TRAQUAIR HOUSE CHARITABLE TRUST

45(A) JAMES SCOULER

Charles Stuart, 7th Earl of Traquair (1746–1827) 1773

Watercolour on ivory, set in gilt-metal frame (top left); 3.8cm (1½in) high; signed and dated at lower right: *Scouler 1773*

James Scouler (1740–1812) was a talented Scottish miniaturist working in London. This was probably painted in 1773 to mark the sitter's marriage to Mary, daughter of George Ravenscroft of Wickham [45(H)].

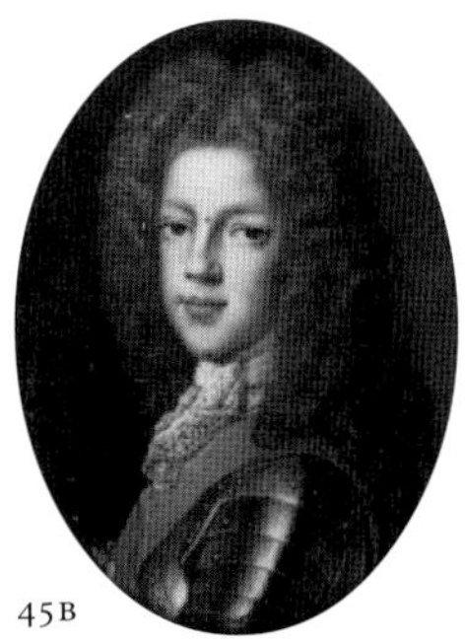

45B

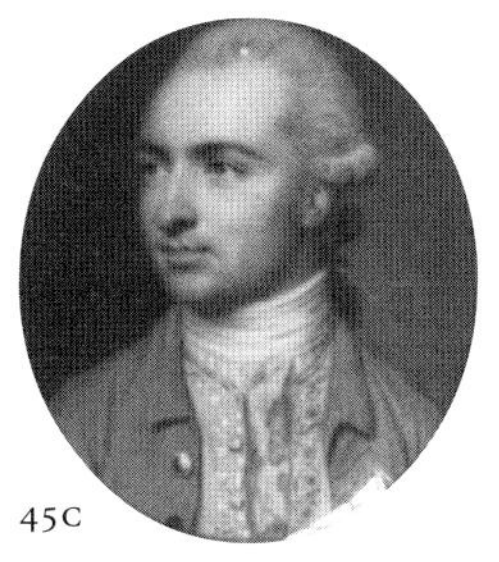

45C

45(B) ANNE CHERON AFTER ALEXIS-SIMON BELLE

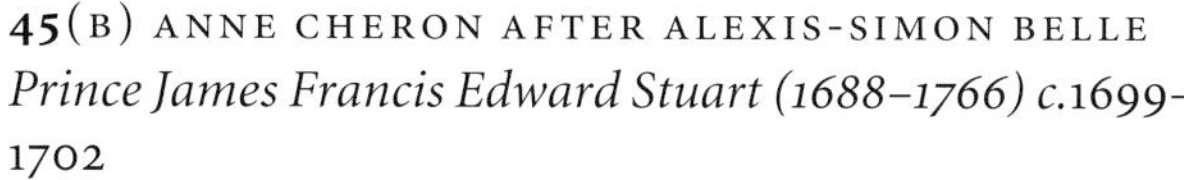

Prince James Francis Edward Stuart (1688–1766) c.1699–1702

Bodycolour on vellum, set in gilt-metal frame (middle of top row); 6.4cm (2½in) high

45(C) JOHN SMART

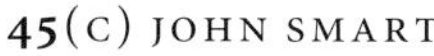

Charles Stuart, 7th Earl of Traquair (1746–1827) c.1773

Watercolour on ivory, set in gilt-metal and diamond frame (top right); 3.8cm (1½in) high

John Smart (1742/3–1811) was, together with George Engleheart and Richard Cosway, one of the leading miniaturists working in London between 1760 and 1810.

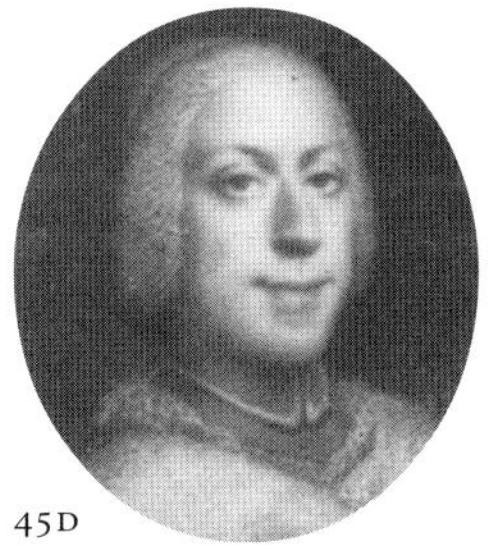

45D

45(D) UNKNOWN ARTIST
AFTER LOUIS-GABRIEL BLANCHET

Prince Henry Benedict Clement Stuart, as Cardinal York (1725–1807) c.1748–50

Watercolour on ivory, set in gilt-metal frame with crown surmount (left of middle row); 3.8cm (1½in) high

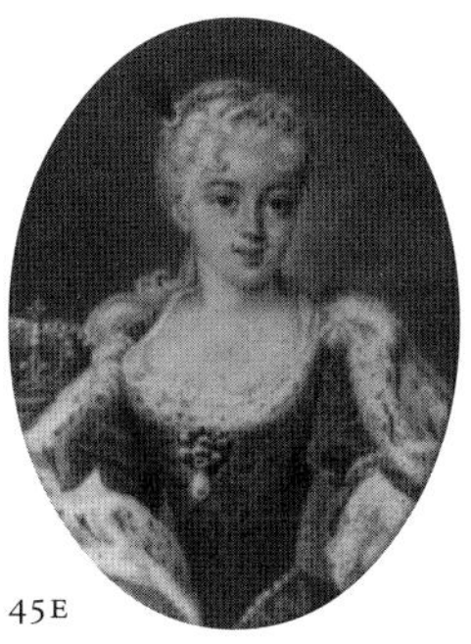

45E

45(E) UNKNOWN ARTIST
AFTER MARTIN VAN MEYTENS

Princess Maria Clementina Sobieska (1702–1735) c.1725

Watercolour on ivory, set in gilt-metal frame (centre of middle row); 8.8cm (3½in) high

45(F) UNKNOWN ARTIST
AFTER MAURICE-QUENTIN DE LA TOUR

Prince Charles Edward Stuart (1720–1788) c.1748–50

Watercolour on ivory, set in gilt-metal frame with crown surmount (right of middle row); 3.8cm (1½in) high

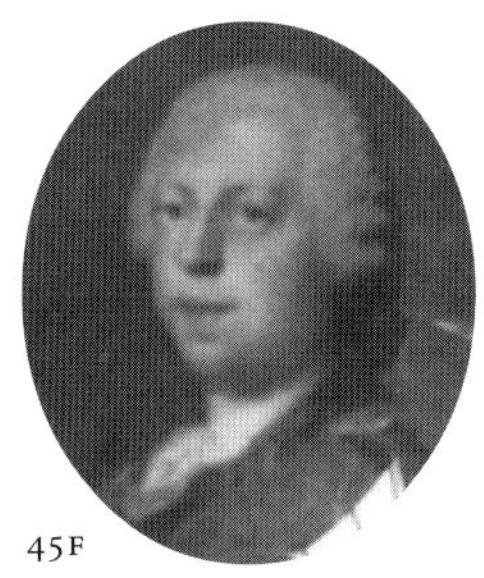

45F

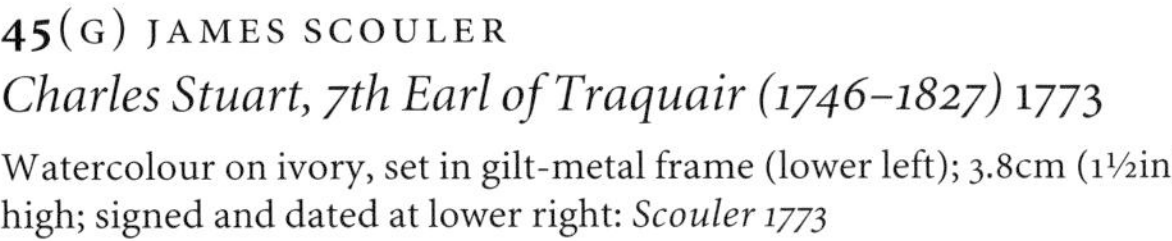

45(G) JAMES SCOULER

Charles Stuart, 7th Earl of Traquair (1746–1827) 1773

Watercolour on ivory, set in gilt-metal frame (lower left); 3.8cm (1½in) high; signed and dated at lower right: *Scouler 1773*

45(H) UNKNOWN BRITISH ARTIST

Mary Ravenscroft, Countess of Traquair (d.1796) c.1773

Watercolour on ivory, set in gilt-metal frame (second from left in lower row); 3.8cm (1½in) high

45(I) JOHN SMART

Lady Lucy Stuart (fl.1750–after 1778) 1773

Watercolour on ivory, set in gilt-metal frame (second from right in lower row); 3.8cm (1½in) high; signed and dated at lower right: *J.S. / 1773*

The sitter, who died unmarried, was the youngest child of John Stuart, 6th Earl of Traquair (1699–1779) [45(J)].

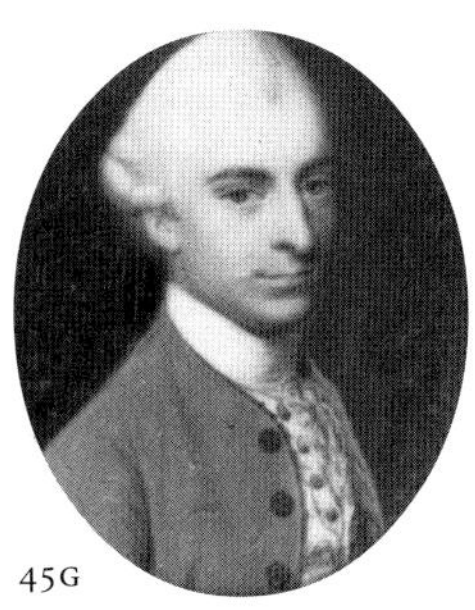

45G

45(J) UNKNOWN SCOTTISH ARTIST
AFTER WILLIAM MILLAR

John Stuart, 6th Earl of Traquair (1669–1779) c.1770

Watercolour on ivory, set in gilt-metal frame (lower right); 3.8cm (1½in) high

A head-and-shoulders portrait in oils of this sitter, previously attributed to Sir George Chalmers, but which is more like the work of William Millar (fl.1751–84) is at Traquair House.

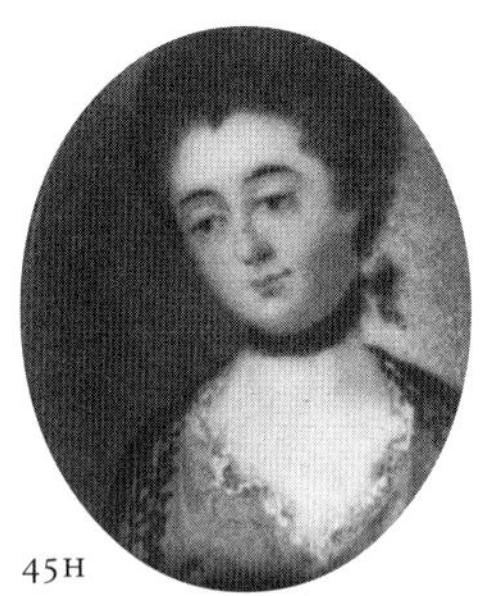

45H

46 UNKNOWN SCOTTISH ARTIST

An Unknown Gentleman, probably Robert MacMurray c.1760–70

Watercolour on ivory, set in turned pearwood frame, oval; 5.1cm (2½in) high; inscribed in pen and ink on paper on verso: *According to family / tradition this / is Robert MacMurray / lawyer of Edinburgh / father of JM / founder of the firm*

COLLECTIONS: by family descent
REFERENCES: Zachs 1998, pl.2a
EXHIBITED: Edinburgh 1999, p.56, no.19

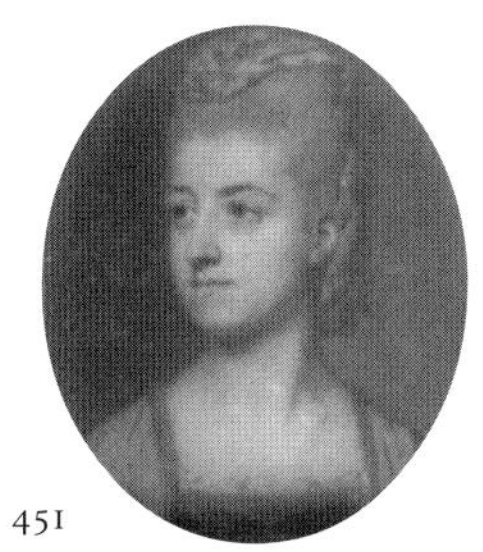
45I

This miniature, which can be dated to the 1760s on the grounds of the sitter's dress and wig, as well as the tightly-drawn style, can be linked to similar works such as *John Stuart, 6th Earl of Traquair* [45(J)] and *William Cadell of Cockenzie* [47]. Miniatures such as these foreshadow the early works by Raeburn and Skirving produced in the 1770s. The lawyer Robert MacMurray was the father of *Elizabeth MacMurray, Mrs James Gilliland* [56] and John Murray I, the eminent Edinburgh-born bookseller, who founded the successful publishing firm in London.

JOHN MURRAY

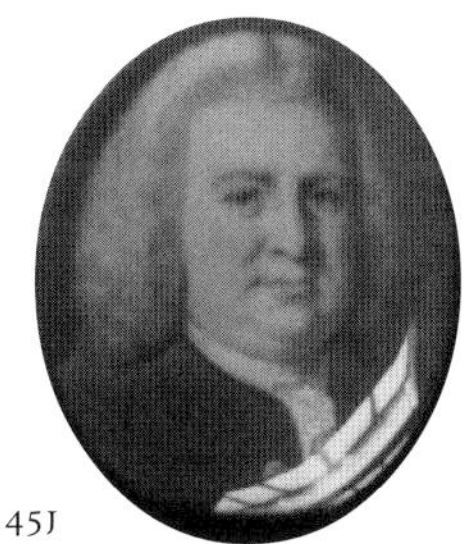
45J

47 UNKNOWN SCOTTISH ARTIST

William Cadell of Cockenzie (c.1699–1777) c.1760–70

Watercolour on ivory, set in gilt-metal frame; 2.5cm (1in) high; engraved on verso: *Willm. Cadell / of Cockenzie / Died March 1777 / Aged 78. / Christian Cadell / relect of Thos. Edington / Died 10 Decr. 1814. / aged 72*
COLLECTIONS: by family descent
EXHIBITED: Edinburgh 1999, p.56, no.18

This miniature, with its careful drawing and muted colouring, may be compared to similarly painted works from the 1760s, such as *An Unknown Gentleman, probably Robert MacMurray* [46] and *John Stuart, 6th Earl of Traquair* [45J].

MAJOR MALCOLM R.S. MACRAE, SKAILL HOUSE, ORKNEY

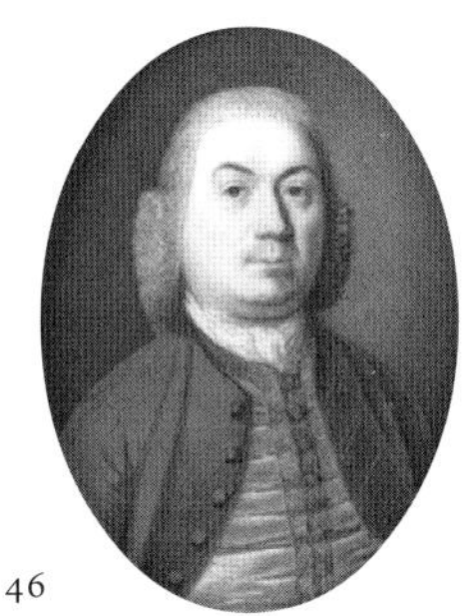
46

48 GERVASE SPENCER

Alexander, 9th Earl of Home (d.1786) 1763

Watercolour on ivory, set in gilt-metal frame; 4.5 cm (1¾in) high; signed with initial on recto: *GS*; inscribed on verso: *Honble Alexander Home afterwards 9th Earl of Home*
COLLECTIONS: by family descent
EXHIBITED: Edinburgh 1951, no.107

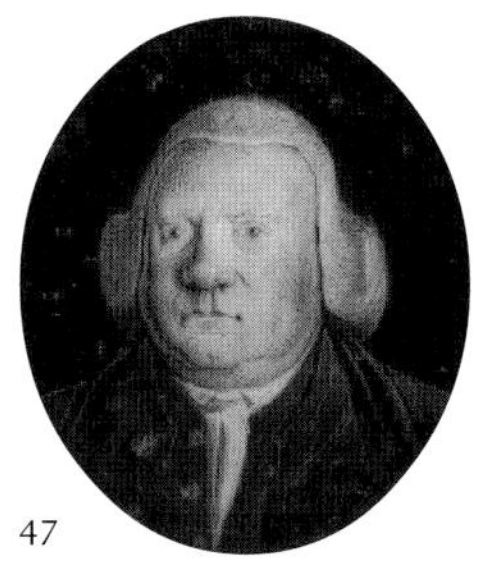

47

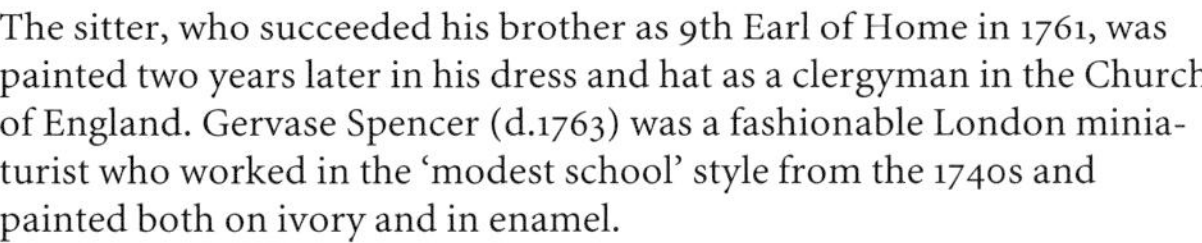

The sitter, who succeeded his brother as 9th Earl of Home in 1761, was painted two years later in his dress and hat as a clergyman in the Church of England. Gervase Spencer (d.1763) was a fashionable London miniaturist who worked in the 'modest school' style from the 1740s and painted both on ivory and in enamel.

THE EARL OF HOME CVO CBE

49 SAMUEL COTES

Archibald, 9th Duke of Hamilton and 6th Duke of Brandon (1740–1819) 1765

Watercolour on ivory, set in gilt-metal frame, with plaited hair under glass on verso; 3.7cm (1½in) high; signed and dated on recto: *S. Cotes pixt / 1765*
COLLECTIONS: by family descent

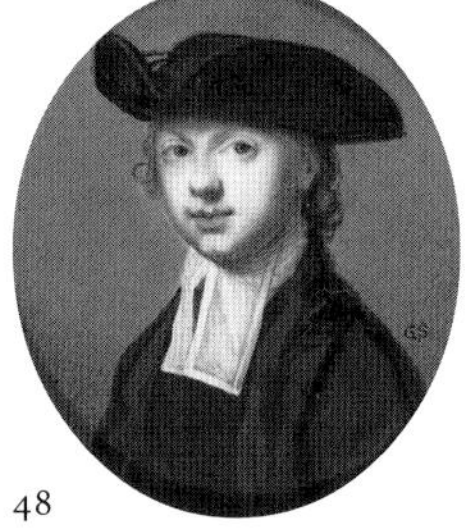

48

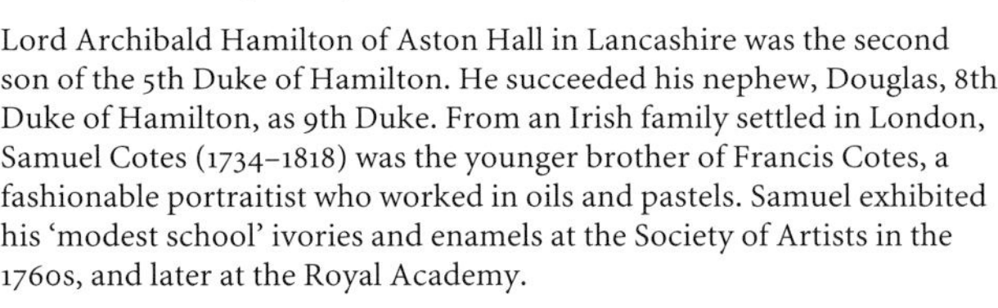

Lord Archibald Hamilton of Aston Hall in Lancashire was the second son of the 5th Duke of Hamilton. He succeeded his nephew, Douglas, 8th Duke of Hamilton, as 9th Duke. From an Irish family settled in London, Samuel Cotes (1734–1818) was the younger brother of Francis Cotes, a fashionable portraitist who worked in oils and pastels. Samuel exhibited his 'modest school' ivories and enamels at the Society of Artists in the 1760s, and later at the Royal Academy.

IN THE COLLECTION OF LENNOXLOVE HOUSE, HADDINGTON (BY KIND PERMISSION OF THE DUKE OF HAMILTON AND BRANDON)

50 PENELOPE CARWARDINE

Elizabeth Gunning, Duchess of Hamilton and Brandon, later Duchess of Argyll (1734–1790) c.1760–5

Watercolour on ivory, set in gilt-metal frame; 3.8cm (1½in) high; engraved on verso: *Elizabeth / Dutchess [sic] of / Hamilton*
COLLECTIONS: by family descent

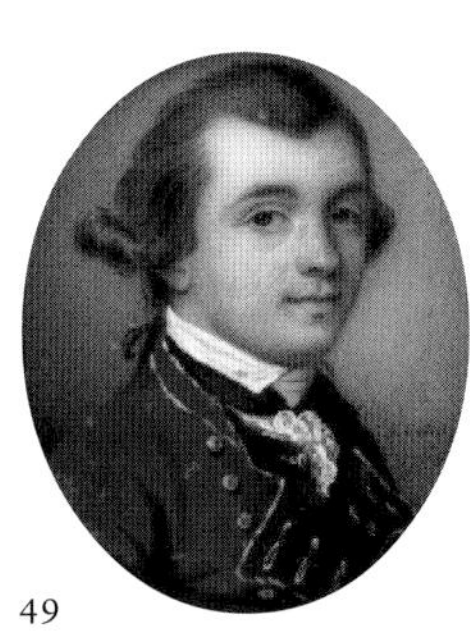

49

In 1752 the sitter, who was one of the two famous Gunning sisters, married James, 6th Duke of Hamilton and 3rd Duke of Brandon. In 1759 she married John Campbell, 5th Duke of Argyll. She was portrayed by Gavin Hamilton in a well-known full-length portrait, dated 1758, now at Lennoxlove House. Penelope Carwardine (*c.*1730–1801) painted most of

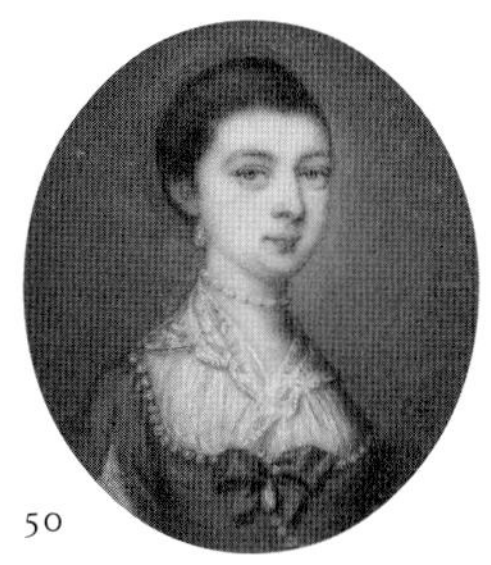

50

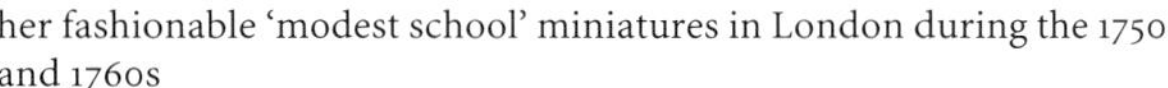

her fashionable 'modest school' miniatures in London during the 1750s and 1760s

IN THE COLLECTION OF LENNOXLOVE HOUSE, HADDINGTON (BY KIND PERMISSION OF THE DUKE OF HAMILTON AND BRANDON)

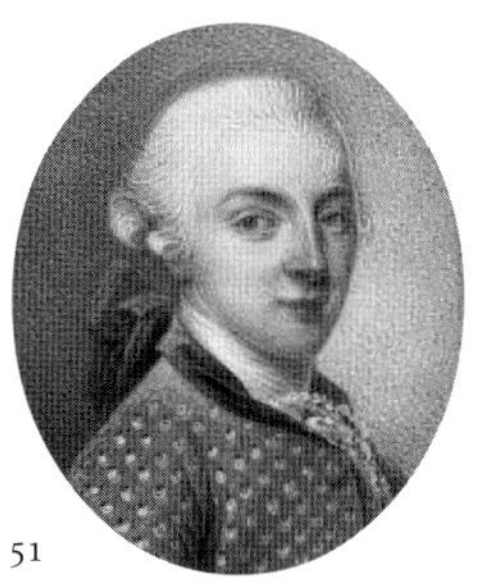

51

51 ATTRIBUTED TO JEAN-ETIENNE LIOTARD

*Francis Charteris of Amisfield, later 7th Earl of Wemyss (1725–1808) c.*1760–5

Watercolour on vellum, set in gold-mounted green aventurine closing locket; 3.8cm (1½in) high
COLLECTIONS: by family descent

The sitter became the 7th Earl of Wemyss in 1787. He was also portrayed in miniature by Ozias Humphry in 1771 and by Richard Cosway in 1779 [59]. This portrait miniature, datable by the sitter's dress and wig, was made in the early 1760s. It is very close in style to the finely detailed portrait miniatures of the itinerant Genevan-born artist Jean-Etienne Liotard.

THE EARL OF WEMYSS AND MARCH KT

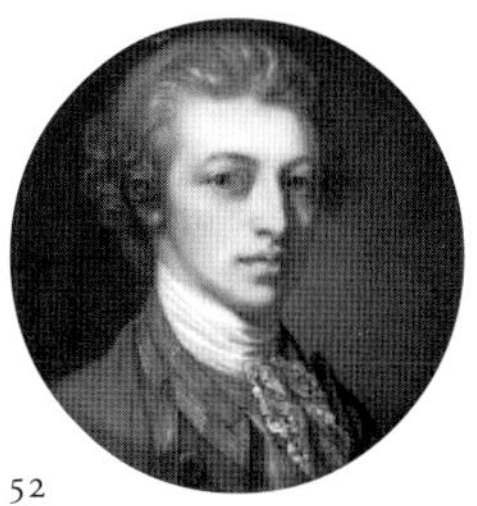

52

52 RICHARD COSWAY
AFTER JEAN-BAPTISTE GREUZE

*The Hon. Campbell Scott (1747–1766) c.*1766–7

Watercolour on ivory, set in scroll-topped gilt-metal frame; 5.8cm (2¼in) dia.; signed with monogram on recto: *RC*
COLLECTIONS: by family descent
REFERENCES: Lloyd 2005, pp.36–7, no.2

The sitter, who was the younger brother of Henry, 3rd Duke of Buccleuch, was the son of Francis, Earl of Dalkeith, and his wife Caroline, Baroness Greenwich, eldest daughter of the 2nd Duke of Argyll. The miniature, as well as another larger oval version (Buccleuch Collection), was copied by Cosway as a family memorial after an oil portrait by Jean-Baptiste Greuze (Private Collection). The portrait had been painted just before the unexpected death of the sitter in Paris, where he and his brother were studying with their tutor Adam Smith, the celebrated political economist.

THE EARL OF HOME CVO CBE

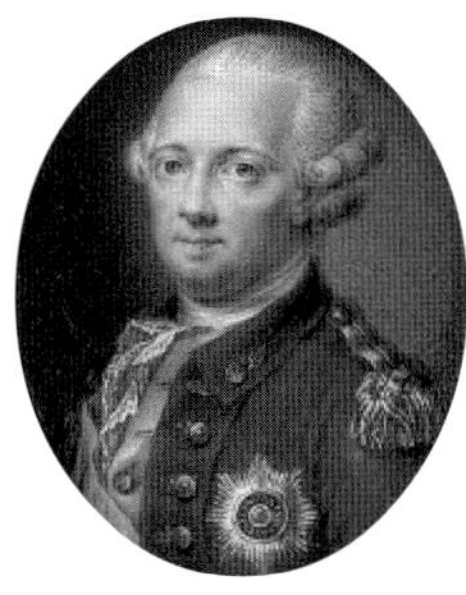

53 UNKNOWN GERMAN ARTIST AFTER ANTON GRAFF

Sir Robert Murray Keith of Murrayshall (1730–1795)
*c.*1770

Watercolour on ivory, set in gold bracelet locket; 3.8cm (1½in) high
COLLECTIONS: by family descent
REFERENCES: *ODNB* 2004

The sitter, who was a diplomat and army officer, was the eldest child of the diplomat Robert Keith of Craig, Kincardineshire, and his wife Margaret Cunningham. After seeing active service on the Continent during the Seven Years War, he was made envoy-extraordinary to the court of Saxony at Dresden in 1769, where he stayed for two years. This miniature was copied from an untraced three-quarter length oil by Anton Graff dated 1770, in which he was shown wearing the uniform of the 87th Highlanders (engraved in Vienna by J. Mansfeld in 1779 and J. Jacobé in 1783). In 1772 Keith was appointed a Knight of the Bath and made envoy-extraordinary to the imperial court in Vienna, a post he held for the next twenty years. He was the brother of Anne Murray Keith [42, 84].

PRIVATE COLLECTION

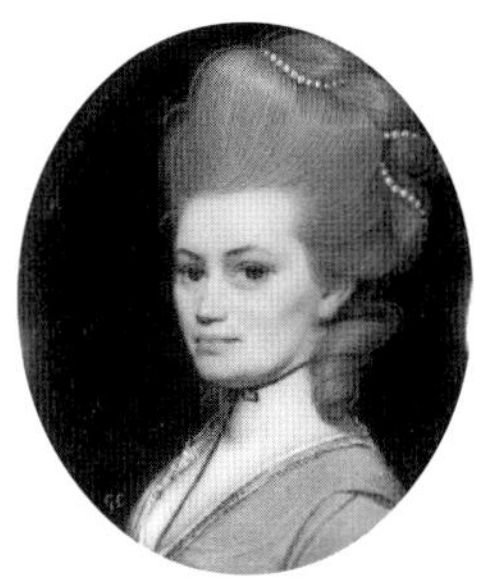

54 GEORGE ENGLEHEART

*Mrs Bazett c.*1770–5

Watercolour on ivory, set in gold locket frame; 3.9cm (1½in) high; signed with initials on recto: *GE*
COLLECTIONS: probably given to the sitter's friend Maria, Countess of Crawford, daughter of Lady Muncaster, wife of John, 1st Baron Muncaster; by family descent
EXHIBITED: Edinburgh 1999, p.57, no.29

This is particularly penetrating and well preserved early miniature painted by George Engleheart (1750/3–1829), who enjoyed a prolific career in London from the early 1770s until the 1810s.

PRIVATE COLLECTION

55 SIR HENRY RAEBURN

James Gilliland (fl.1730–90) c.1775

See pages 46 and 47

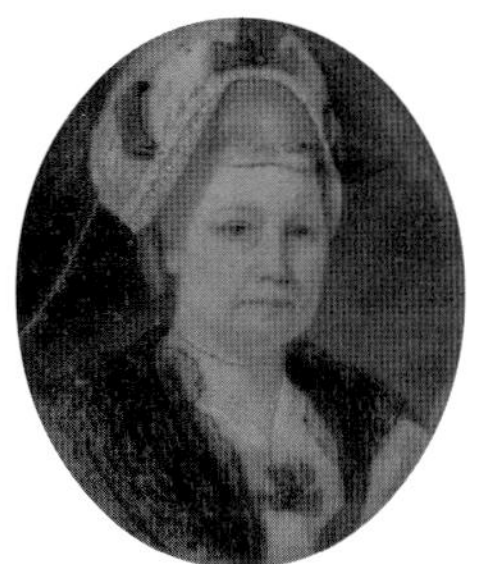

56 SIR HENRY RAEBURN

Elizabeth MacMurray, Mrs James Gilliland c.1775

Watercolour on ivory (cracked), set in gilt-metal frame, 3.9cm (1½in) high
COLLECTIONS: by family descent
REFERENCES: Zachs 1998, ill.
EXHIBITED: Edinburgh & London 1997–8 (London only) Edinburgh 1999, p.57, no.27

The sitter was the daughter of the Edinburgh lawyer Robert MacMurray [46], and the sister of the bookseller John Murray I, the founder of the famous London publishing house. This miniature and its pair of the sitter's husband, the Edinburgh goldsmith *James Gilliland* [55], are key works for establishing the early career of Raeburn as a miniaturist in Edinburgh during the 1770s.

JOHN MURRAY

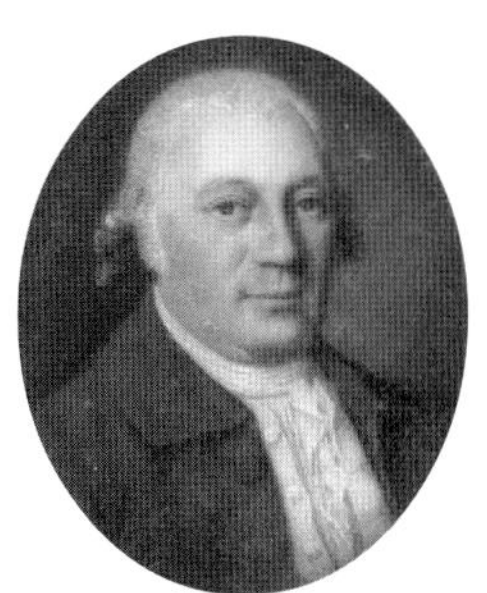

57 SIR HENRY RAEBURN

Andrew Wood (1742–1821) c.1775–80

Watercolour on ivory, set in gold bracelet locket, with plaited hair set under glass compartment on verso, with velvet attached; 3.8cm (1½in) high
COLLECTIONS: Mrs Edmonstoune, 5 Great Stuart Street, Edinburgh (in 1876); Miss Edmonstoune (in 1901); presented to a friend; by family descent
REFERENCES: Armstrong *et al.* 1901, opp.p.4, pl.II(B) and pp.38 and 114; Greig 1911
EXHIBITED: Edinburgh 1876, p.38, no.306

In 1901 Sir Walter Armstrong described this miniature of the Edinburgh surgeon Andrew Wood by Raeburn as having been painted 'without the grace of Cosway or the grandeur in little of Samuel Cooper, but it shows that its author could see character and avoid irrelevance, and that he was gifted with that downright trust in sincerity on which all great art is built' (Armstrong *et al.* 1901, p.38).

PRIVATE COLLECTION

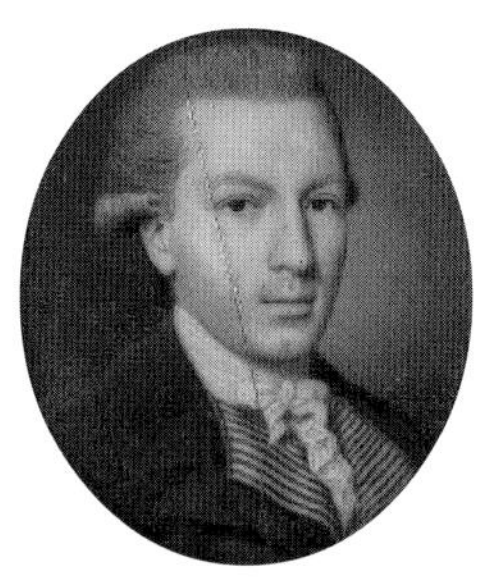

58 SIR HENRY RAEBURN

*George Sandilands of Strathtyrum (1755–1824) c.*1775

Watercolour on ivory (cracked), set in gilt-wood frame, 3.9cm (1½in) high
COLLECTIONS: by family descent
EXHIBITED: Edinburgh & London 1997–8; Edinburgh 1999, p.57, no.28

This miniature was first attributed to Raeburn by Richard Walker and can be connected to the careful draughtsmanship and colouring seen in the portraits of *James Gilliland* [55], *Mrs James Gilliland* [56] and *Andrew Wood* [57], all datable to the mid- and late 1770s.

PRIVATE COLLECTION

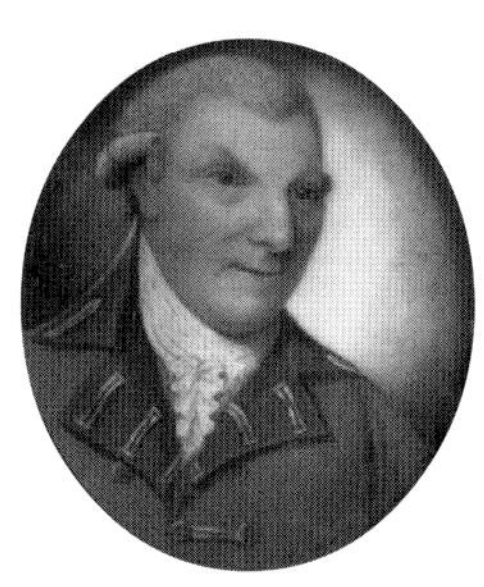

59 RICHARD COSWAY

Francis Charteris of Amisfield, later 7th Earl of Wemyss (1725–1809) 1779

See pages 48 and 49

60 UNKNOWN SCOTTISH ARTIST AFTER DAVID MARTIN

*William Nisbet of Dirleton (1724–1783) c.*1782

Watercolour on ivory, set in turned wooden frame, 3.8cm (1½in) high
COLLECTIONS: by family descent
EXHIBITED: Edinburgh 1999, p.78, no.173

William Nisbet, who was a significant landowner in East Lothian, is shown wearing the coat of the Caledonian Hunt. This miniature is copied from an oil portrait of the sitter by David Martin (1737–1798), which was painted in 1782 (Private Collection). The unknown miniaturist was a Scottish contemporary of Skirving and Raeburn.

PRIVATE COLLECTION

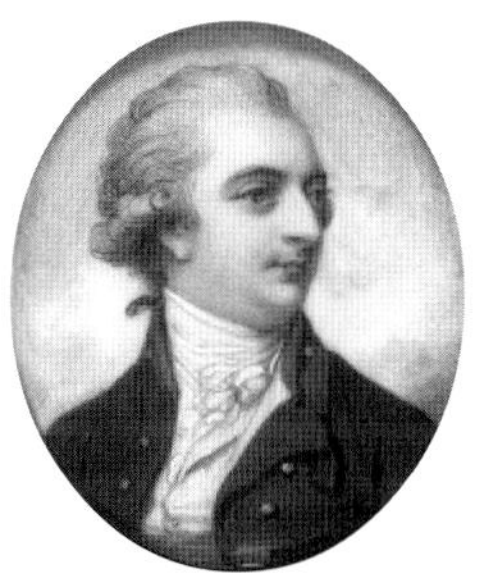

61 RICHARD COSWAY

Thomas, Viscount Wentworth of Wellesborough (1745–1815) c.1780–5

Watercolour on ivory, set in oval gold locket, mounted within rectangular black lacquered wooden frame; 5.8cm (2¼in) high
COLLECTIONS: by family descent
EXHIBITED: Edinburgh & London 1995–6, p.118, no.53 and p.37, col. pl. 27

The sitter, who succeeded to the peerage in 1774, married Mary, Dowager Countess Ligonier of Clonmell in 1788.

PRIVATE COLLECTION

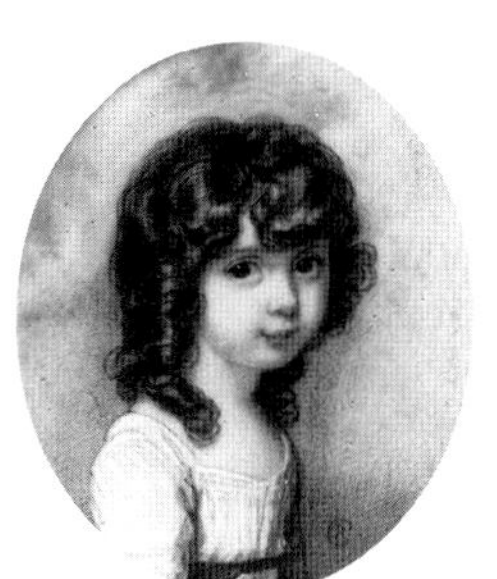

62 RICHARD COSWAY

Jane Margaret Douglas of Douglas, later Baroness Montagu of Boughton (b.1779) 1784

Watercolour on ivory, set in gilt-metal frame; 4.5cm (1¾in) high; signed with monogram on recto: *RC*
COLLECTIONS: by family descent
EXHIBITED: Edinburgh 1951

The sitter was the daughter of *Archibald Douglas, 1st Baron Douglas of Douglas* [63] by his first wife Lady Lucy Graham. In 1804 she married Henry James Scott, 2nd Baron Montagu of Boughton.

THE EARL OF HOME CVO CBE

63 *recto*

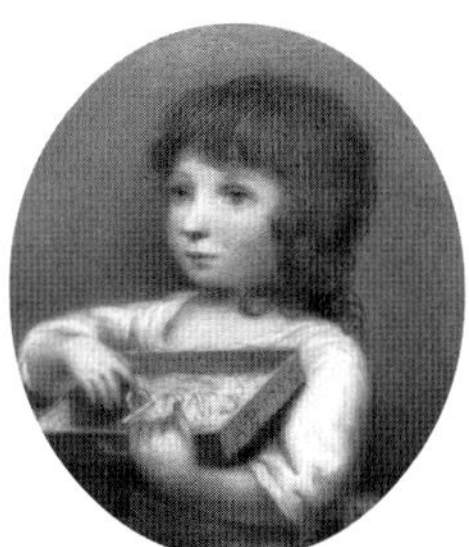

63 *verso*

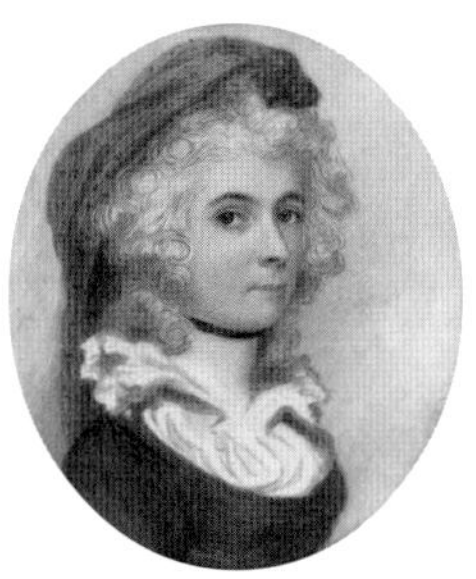

63 ANDREW PLIMER

Archibald Douglas, 1st Baron Douglas of Douglas (1748–1827) [recto]; *his daughter Caroline Lucy Douglas, later Lady Scott (1784–1857)* [verso] 1786

Watercolour on ivory, set in gold frame with enamel decoration; 3.9cm (1½in) high; signed with initials and dated on side of tray on verso: *A P 1786*
COLLECTIONS: by family descent

Archibald Douglas was the successful claimant in the famous 'Douglas' claim – a legal battle for the title Baron Douglas. Caroline Lucy Douglas, the second daughter of Lord Douglas, married Admiral Sir George Scott in 1810. Andrew Plimer (1763–1837), who was a pupil of Richard Cosway, was one of the most successful and prolific miniaturists working in London during the late eighteenth and early nineteenth centuries. He exhibited his work at the Royal Academy from 1786 to 1830.

THE EARL OF HOME CVO CBE

64 ANDREW PLIMER

Martha Whyte, Countess of Elgin and Kincardine (c.1740–1810) c.1790

Watercolour on ivory, set in gilt-metal frame; 6.9cm (2¾in) high
COLLECTIONS: by family descent
REFERENCES: Checkland 1988, ill. opp. p.66, col. pl.1

In 1759 Martha Whyte, who was born into a family of London bankers, married Charles Bruce, 5th Earl of Elgin and 9th Earl of Kincardine. The third of their eight children was Thomas Bruce, 7th Earl of Elgin and 11th Earl of Kincardine, and was famous for his embassy to Constantinople and acquisition of classical Greek sculptures from Athens [74, 79].

THE EARL OF ELGIN AND KINCARDINE KT

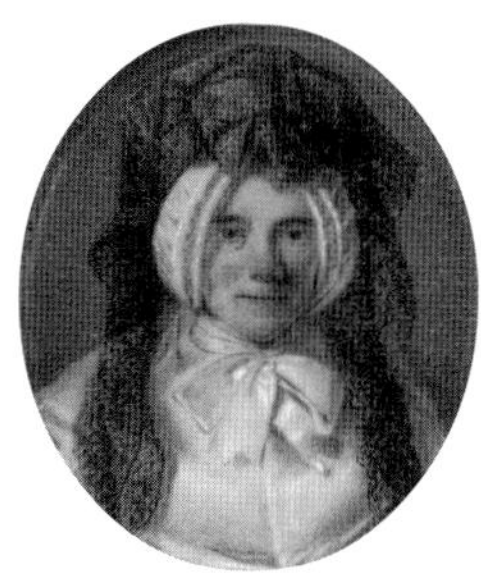

65 ARCHIBALD SKIRVING

Euphan Guthrie, Mrs Charles Wright of Shallope (1739–1831) either c.1784–6 or c.1796–1803

Watercolour on ivory, set in ornamented gilt-metal brooch; 4.2cm (1½in) high
COLLECTIONS: by family descent
EXHIBITED: Edinburgh 1999, p.72, no.132

The sitter was a friend of Florence Nightingale. Skirving painted this finely detailed miniature and a similarly posed rectangular pastel of her either during the mid-1780s or the very early nineteenth century. A photograph of the pastel (untraced) is in the archive of the Scottish National Portrait Gallery, Edinburgh.

MAJOR MALCOLM R.S. MACRAE, SKAILL HOUSE, ORKNEY

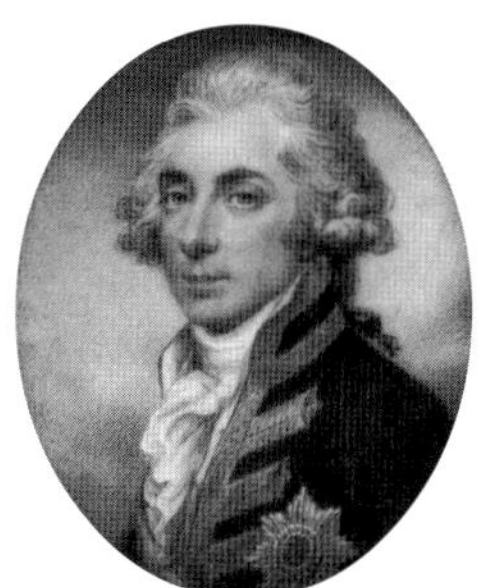

66 PHILIP JEAN

George Keith Elphinstone, Viscount Keith (1746–1823) c.1787

Watercolour on ivory, set in gilt-metal frame; 7.6cm (3in) high; inscribed on verso: *Admiral Visct. Keith*
COLLECTIONS: by family descent

The famous admiral, George Keith Elphinstone, was the fourth son of Charles, 10th Baron Elphinstone. A key moment in his naval career was his capture of the Dutch fortress at Muizenberg at the Cape of Good Hope in 1795. In 1787 Admiral Keith married Jane, daughter and heiress of Colonel William Mercer, by whom he had a daughter, Margaret [85], who succeeded as Baroness Keith and Nairn. His sister was Clementina Elizabeth Elphinstone [77], who married *James Drummond, Baron Perth and Lord Drummond of Stobhall* [72]. Admiral Keith is shown in uniform, wearing the Order of the Bath, and this miniature is likely to have painted as a marriage portrait.

PRIVATE COLLECTION

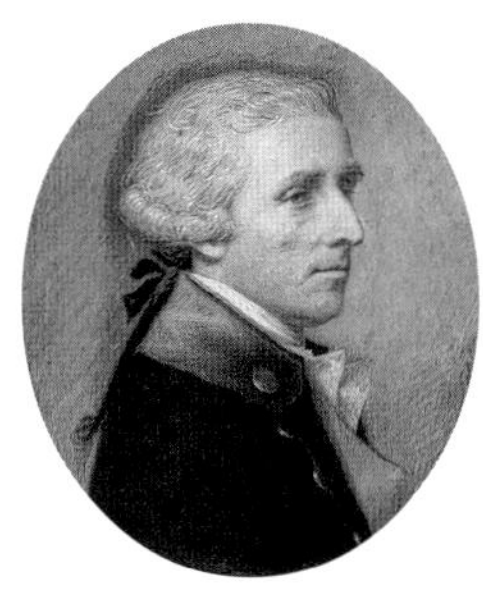

67 UNKNOWN ARTIST AFTER HUGH DOUGLAS HAMILTON

Sir William Hamilton (1730–1803) c.1789–90

Watercolour on ivory, set in a gilt-metal frame; 6.9cm (2¾in); cartouche engraved: *SIR W. HAMILTON*; inscribed in pen and ink on verso: *122 / Sir W Hamilton / 436*
COLLECTIONS: by family descent
REFERENCES: London 1996, pp.262–4, nos.162–3 and pp.295–6, no.185

The sitter was a famous diplomat, collector and antiquarian, who was the British representative to the court at Naples from 1764 to 1800. His second marriage was to Emma Hart, and her subsequent liaison with Admiral Nelson attracted European notice. This miniature, which is of high quality and was formerly attributed to Horace Hone, was most probably painted by a British artist in Italy. It is very closely related to the small oil on canvas of the diplomat painted by Hugh Douglas Hamilton (1740–1808), the noted Irish portraitist working in oils and pastels, which also hangs at Lennoxlove House. A line engraving of the oil was made around 1790 in Naples by Guglielmo Morghen.

IN THE COLLECTION OF LENNOXLOVE HOUSE, HADDINGTON (BY KIND PERMISSION OF THE DUKE OF HAMILTON AND BRANDON)

68 SAMUEL SHELLEY

Douglas Hamilton, 8th Duke of Hamilton and 5th Duke of Brandon (1756–1799) c.1790

See pages 50 and 51

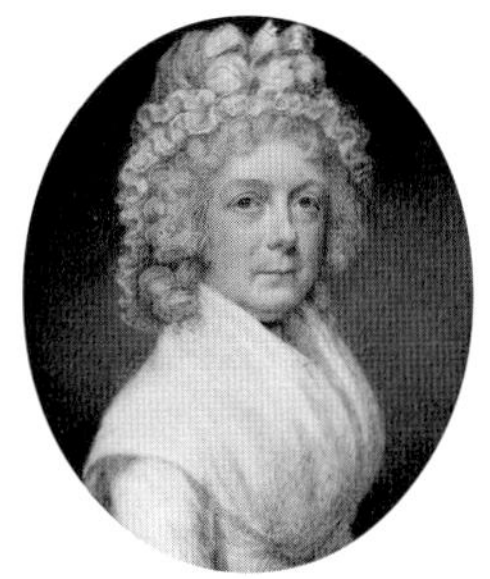

69 PHILIP JEAN

Anne Dalrymple, Countess of Balcarres (1727–1820) c.1790

Watercolour on ivory, set in gilt-metal frame; 6.8cm (2¾ins); inscribed in pen and ink on verso: *Lady Balcarres*
COLLECTIONS: D.S. Lavender (Antiques) Ltd, London
REFERENCES: Edinburgh & London 1992–3, pp.106 and 114
EXHIBITED: Edinburgh 1999, p.70, no.118

The sitter was the daughter of Sir Robert Dalrymple of Castleton, by Anne, daughter of Sir William Cunningham, Bt, of Caprington. In 1749 she married James, 5th Earl of Balcarres, and they had eleven children, including Lady Anne Lindsay (later Barnard), the author of the song 'Auld Robin Gray'. The Jersey-born artist Philip Jean (1755–1802) exhibited his miniatures at the Royal Academy from 1787 until his death. This work is a notable example of his confident brushwork and skilful handling of character.

PRIVATE COLLECTION

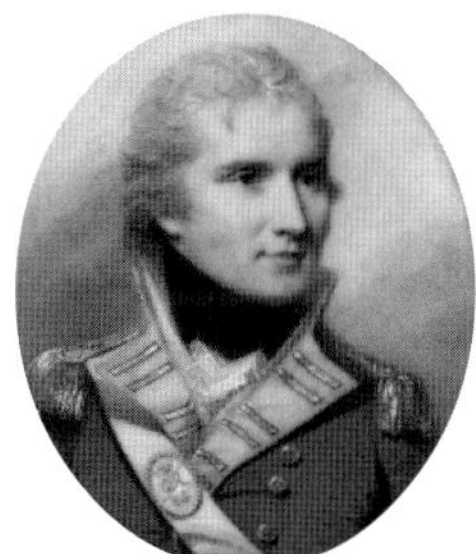

70 GEORGE ENGLEHEART

General Sir Ronald Craufurd Ferguson (1773–1841) 1794

Watercolour on ivory, set in gilt-metal frame with plaited hair on verso, set in original red leather closing case; 7.9cm (3⅛in) high; painted on badge of uniform: *GR 84*; typed label on verso: *Englehart.* [*sic*]; inscribed at base of frame on recto: *Sir Ronald Ferguson by Englehart* [*sic*]; inscribed at base on verso: *Sir Ronald Ferguson 1794*
COLLECTIONS: by family descent

The sitter, who was a distinguished soldier, was the second son of William Ferguson of Raith and Jean, daughter of Robert Craufurd of Restalrig. He joined the army as an ensign in the 53rd Regiment in 1790, and served with Wellington in the Peninsular War. Ferguson was promoted to Lieutenant-General in 1813, and full General in 1830. Ferguson – a noted Whig – was MP for Kirkcaldy from 1806 to 1830 and for Nottingham from 1830 until his death. He married Jean, the natural daughter of General Sir Hector Munro of Novar in 1798. Two of their children, Jane and Robert, were portrayed by Alexander Gallaway in 1805 [78]. This miniature was painted in 1794, when Ferguson was promoted to Lieutenant-Colonel of the 84th Regiment, and before he set off the following year to serve in India. This is good example of the mature style of miniature painting by George Engleheart (1750/3–1829) from the 1790s.

PRIVATE COLLECTION

71 ARCHIBALD SKIRVING
Charles-Philippe, Comte d'Artois, later Charles x (1757–1836) 1796–7

See pages 52 and 53

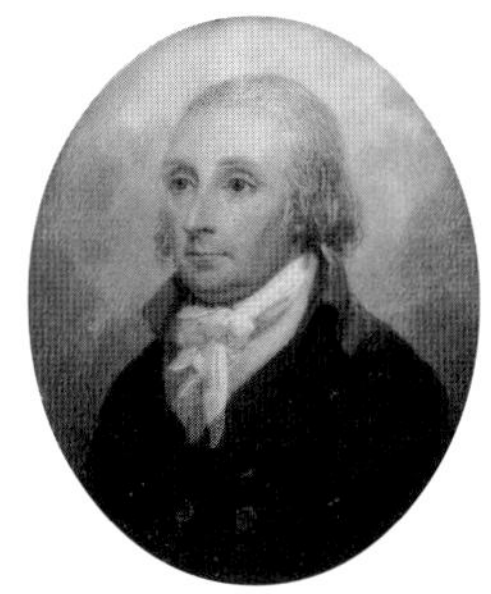

72 ARCHIBALD SKIRVING
James Drummond, Baron Perth and Lord Drummond of Stobhall (1744–1800) 1798

Watercolour on ivory, set in gold frame; 7.4cm (2⅞in) high; engraved around rim on recto: *James Baron Perth 1798*
COLLECTIONS: by family descent
EXHIBITED: Edinburgh 1999, p.71, no.124

James Drummond was the third son of James Lundin – who assumed the name of Drummond – and of his wife Rachael Bruce. As the nearest male relation of James Drummond, 4th Earl and 1st titular Duke of Perth, in 1794 he presented a claim to these titles to the king and the House of Lords. In 1797 he was created a British peer as Baron Perth and Lord Drummond of Stobhall. In 1798 Archibald Skirving (1749–1819) also painted a miniature of Lord Perth's only child, *Clementina Sarah Drummond, later Baroness Willoughby de Eresby* [73].

PRIVATE COLLECTION

73 ARCHIBALD SKIRVING
Clementina Sarah Drummond, later Baroness Willoughby de Eresby (1786–1865) c.1798

See pages 54 and 55

74 RICHARD COSWAY
Thomas Bruce, 7th Earl of Elgin and 11th Earl of Kincardine (1766–1841) 1799

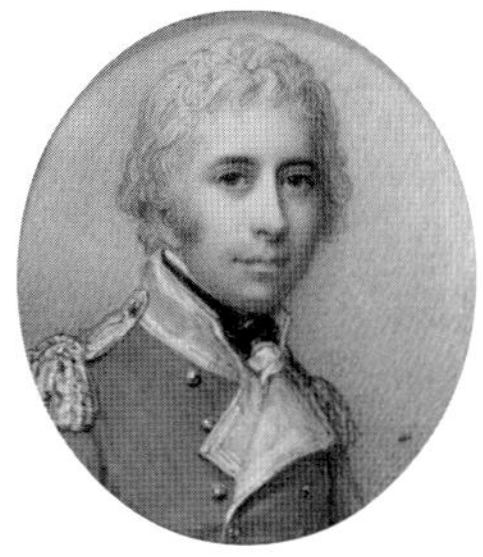

Watercolour on ivory, set in gold locket frame; 7.7cm (3in) high; signed and dated on verso: *Rd. Cosway* R.A. */ Primarius / Pictor / Serenissimi / Walliae / Principis / Pinxit / 1799*
COLLECTIONS: Mary Nisbet of Dirleton, later Countess of Elgin and Kincardine, and later Mrs Robert Ferguson; by family descent
EXHIBITED: Edinburgh 1999, p.78, no.174

The sitter was the famous ambassador to the Sublime Porte in Constantinople and acquirer of the classical Greek marbles from the Parthenon in Athens. This miniature was painted in 1799, the year of his marriage to the heiress Mary Nisbet of Dirleton. Another version of this miniature by Cosway was painted in 1807 to mark the sitter's brief tenure that year as Lord Lieutenant of Fife [79].

PRIVATE COLLECTION

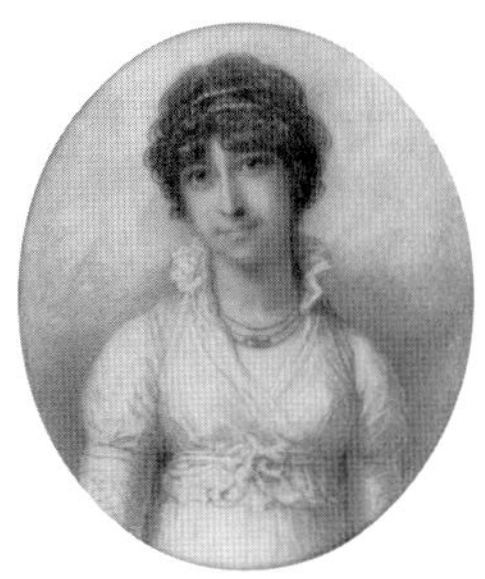

75 RICHARD COSWAY

Lady Charlotte Bruce, later Lady Charlotte Durham (1771–1816) 1799

Watercolour on ivory, set in gilt-metal frame; 7.1cm (2¾in) high; signed and dated in pen and ink on paper inside verso: *Ly. Charte. Durham / Rdus. Cosway R.A. / Primarius Pictor / Serenissimi Walliae / Principis / Pinxit / 1799*

Lady Charlotte Bruce was the youngest daughter of Charles Bruce, 5th Earl of Elgin and 9th Earl of Kincardine. She married Admiral Sir Philip Charles Durham. This is good example of the muted tonality used by Richard Cosway (1742–1821) in his late style of miniature painting.

THE EARL OF ELGIN AND KINCARDINE KT

76 ATTRIBUTED TO ARCHIBALD SKIRVING

Margaret Campbell of Shawfield, later Countess of Wemyss (d.1850) c.1800–1805

Watercolour on ivory, set in the original closing red leather case; 7.9cm (3⅛in) high
COLLECTIONS: by family descent

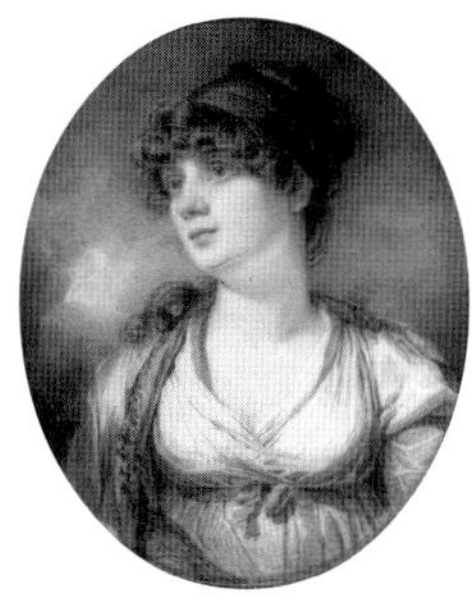

The sitter was the fourth daughter of Walter Campbell of Shawfield by his first wife Eleanor, daughter of Robert Kerr of Newfield. In 1794 she married Francis Wemyss Charteris, later 8th Earl of Wemyss, in Edinburgh. This strongly coloured miniature is relatively unusual for the work of Archibald Skirving (1749–1819) in that his other miniatures are either more densely or more lightly worked. However, the hatching of the painting is similar to his other known works, and this miniature can be understood as a specific response to the colouristic and lighting effects demonstrated by Raeburn in his oil paintings from this date.

THE EARL OF WEMYSS AND MARCH KT

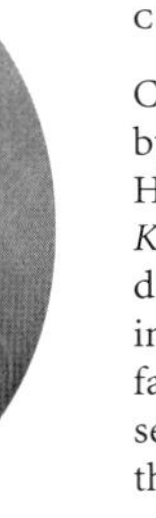

77 ANNE FOLDSONE, MRS JOSEPH MEE

Clementina Elizabeth Elphinstone, Baroness Perth (1749–1822) 1800

Watercolour on ivory, set in gold locket frame, the verso with plaited hair border, and in the centre the initials, *CP*, under a baron's coronet; 7.7cm (3in) high
COLLECTIONS: by family descent

Clementina was the fourth daughter of Charles, 10th Baron Elphinstone, by Clementina, daughter of John Fleming, 6th Earl of Wigton. Her brother was the noted admiral *George Keith Elphinstone, Viscount Keith* [66]. The sitter's husband, James Drummond, Baron Perth [72] died on 2 July 1800, and the mourning dress seen in this miniature would indicate that it was painted soon afterwards. Mrs Mee (1770/5–1851) was a fashionable miniaturist working in London from 1790, who painted a series of cabinet miniatures in 1812–13 for the Prince Regent, known as the 'Gallery of Beauties of George III' (Royal Collection).

PRIVATE COLLECTION

78 ALEXANDER GALLAWAY

Jane Craufurd Ferguson (b.1800) and her brother Robert Munro-Ferguson (1802–1864) 1805

Watercolour on ivory, set in original black lacquered wooden frame with gilt-metal slip; 13 × 10.3cm (5⅛ × 4in); inscribed in pen and ink on verso: *Jane Craufurd Ferguson / Robert Ferguson / Date 1805*
COLLECTIONS: by family descent

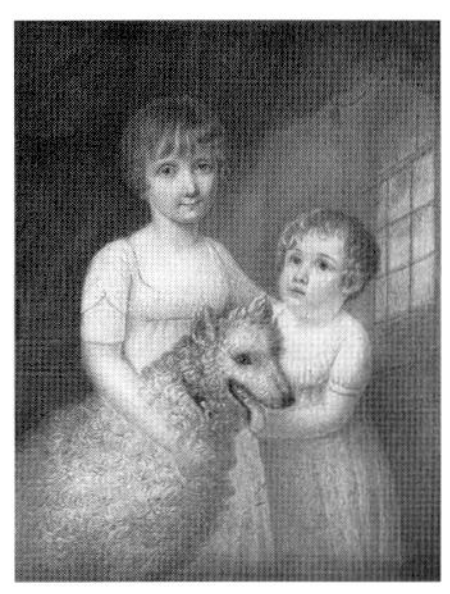

These two sitters were the children of General Sir Ronald Craufurd Ferguson [70] by Jean, natural daughter of General Sir Hector Munro of Novar. The boy made a career as a soldier and was Lieutenant-Colonel of the 79th Highlanders, before becoming MP for Kirkcaldy Burghs from 1841 to 1861. In 1859 he married Emma, daughter of James Henry Mandeville of Merton, Surrey. Alexander Gallaway (fl.1794 – after 1812) began his career as a miniaturist in Glasgow, before working in Edinburgh. This is one of his largest and most ambitious compositions.

PRIVATE COLLECTION

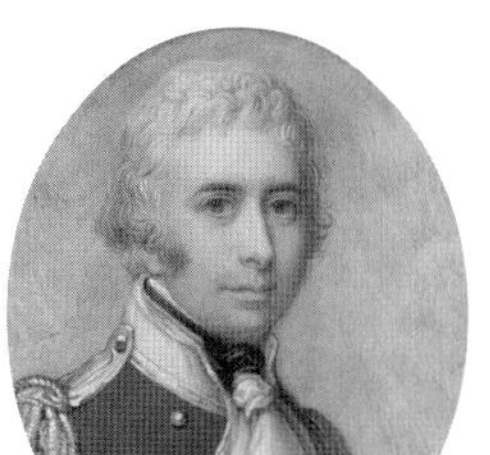

79 RICHARD COSWAY

Thomas Bruce, 7th Earl of Elgin and 11th Earl of Kincardine (1766–1841) 1807

Watercolour on ivory, set in gilt-metal frame; 6.3cm (2½in) high
COLLECTIONS: by family descent
EXHIBITED: Edinburgh & London 1995–6, p.129, no.180, and p.87, col. pl.96

The sitter is shown wearing the uniform of the Lord Lieutenant of Fife, an appointment he held for two months in 1807. The prime version of this miniature was painted in 1799 [74] to mark Lord Elgin's marriage to the heiress Mary Nisbet of Dirleton.

THE EARL OF ELGIN AND KINCARDINE KT

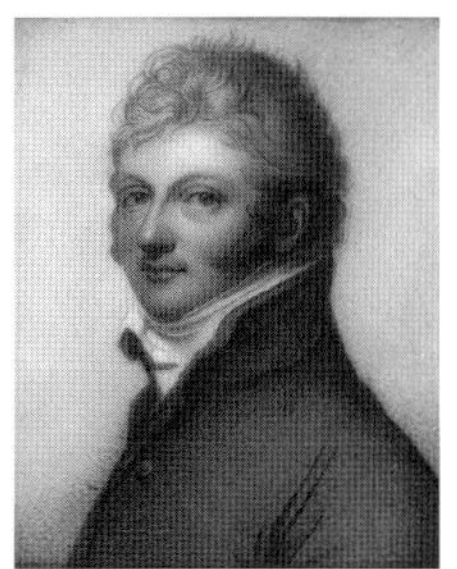

80 HENRY BONE AFTER RICHARD COSWAY

Richard Bingham, 2nd Earl of Lucan (1764–1839) 1808

Enamel on porcelain, set in ormolu frame; 7.6 × 5.1cm (3 × 2in)
COLLECTIONS: by family descent
EXHIBITED: Edinburgh & London 1995–6, p.129, no.183

The sitter married Lady Elizabeth Belasyse, formerly the wife of Bernard Edward Howard (later 12th Duke of Norfolk). One of their daughters, Louisa [87], married Francis Wemyss Charteris Douglas, Lord Elcho, later 9th Earl of Wemyss in Paris in 1817. Cosway's original drawing for this miniature, and another enamel by Bone dated 1812, were sold at Christie's, London, 21 November 2000, lots 92 and 25. Henry Bone

(1755–1834) was the leading enameller in London during the early nineteenth century.

THE EARL OF WEMYSS AND MARCH KT

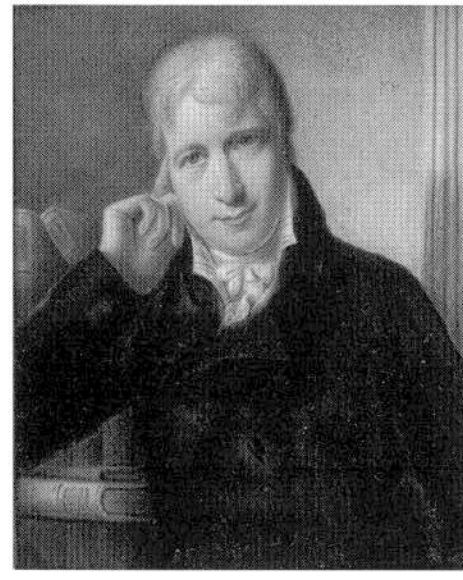

81 ALEXANDER GALLAWAY

An Unknown Gentleman 1809

Watercolour on ivory, set in gilt-metal frame; 7.4 × 5.6cm (2⅞ × 2⅛in); signed and dated on verso: *A. Gallaway / pinxt/ Edin. 6 James's / Square / 1809*
COLLECTIONS: Ellison Fine Art

Alexander Gallaway (fl.1794–after 1812) began his career as a portrait miniaturist in Glasgow, but soon moved to Edinburgh, where his studio was at 6 St James's Square. He exhibited his work at the Associated Society of Artists in Edinburgh from 1808 to 1812. The sitter in this miniature, which was painted in Edinburgh, bears some resemblance to Sir Walter Scott, who is known to have sat to Gallaway a few years earlier. There is a pair to this miniature [82].

PRIVATE COLLECTION

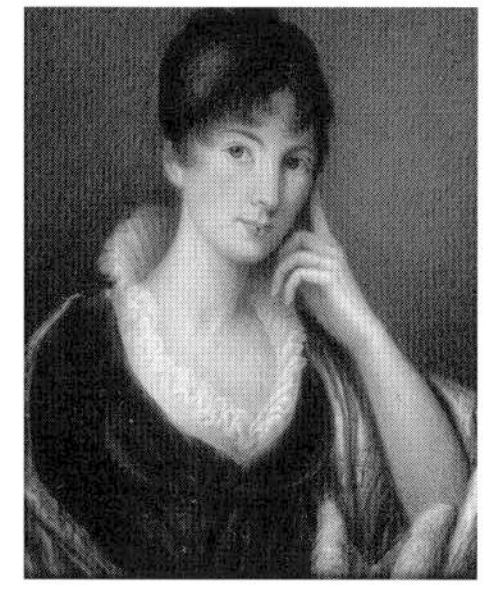

82 ALEXANDER GALLAWAY

An Unknown Lady 1809

Watercolour on ivory, set in gilt-metal frame; 7.4 × 5.6cm (2⅞ × 2⅛in)
COLLECTIONS: Ellison Fine Art

The sitter in this miniature, which is one of a pair [81], bears a resemblance to the wife of Sir Walter Scott, Marguerite Charlotte Charpentier.

PRIVATE COLLECTION

83 ANDREW ROBERTSON AFTER WILLIAM WOOD

Thomas Legge 1810

Watercolour on ivory, set in oval gilt-metal slip within black-lacquered wooden frame; 7.6cm (3in) high; inscribed on verso: *Thomas Legge / by Andrew Robertson / after William Wood / 33 Gerrard Street / London / 1810*
COLLECTIONS: Ellison Fine Art

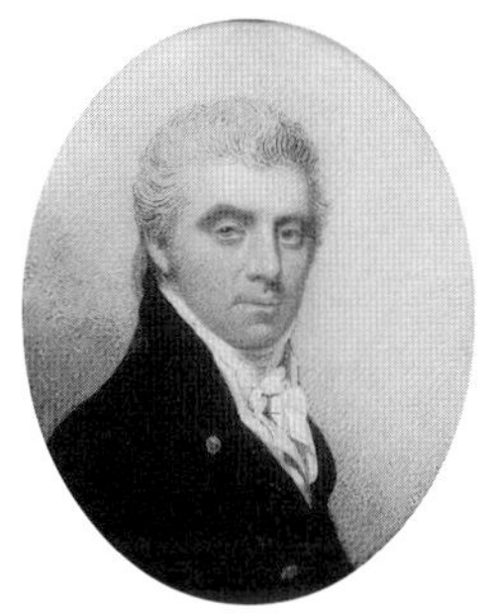

There is a Miss Legge recorded in William Wood's ledger books in the National Art Library at the Victoria & Albert Museum, London. The fact that Mr Legge's name is missing may be because Wood gave the miniature directly to Robertson to keep and copy. William Wood (1769–1810) was a fashionable miniaturist in London, whose style was strongly influenced by that of Richard Cosway. Andrew Robertson (1777–1845), born in Aberdeen, was one of the dominant miniaturists in London during the first half of the nineteenth century.

PRIVATE COLLECTION

84 ANNE FOLDSTONE, MRS JOSEPH MEE
*Mrs Anne Murray Keith (1736–1818) c.*1800–10

See pages 56 and 57

85 GEORGE SANDERS
Margaret Mercer Elphinstone, Baroness Keith and Nairn, later Comtesse de Flahault (1788–1867) 1814

See pages 58 and 59

86 JEAN-BAPTISTE AUGUSTIN
Peter Middleton (b.1786) 1817

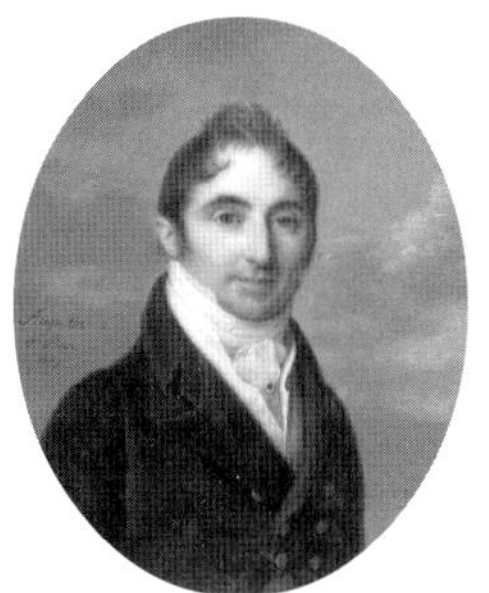

Watercolour on ivory, set in gilt-metal frame, in original leather case; 7.6cm (3in); signed and dated on recto: *Augustin à Paris 1817*
COLLECTIONS: by family descent

Peter Middleton lived at Middleton Lodge, Ilkley, and Stockeld Park in Yorkshire. His daughter, Juliana, married Henry Constable Maxwell Stuart, 16th Laird of Traquair in 1840. Jean-Baptiste Augustin (1759–1832) – together with Jean-Baptiste Isabey (1767–1855) – dominated the French school of miniature painting in the late eighteenth and early nineteenth centuries. This is one of his finest miniatures of a British sitter.

TRAQUAIR HOUSE CHARITABLE TRUST

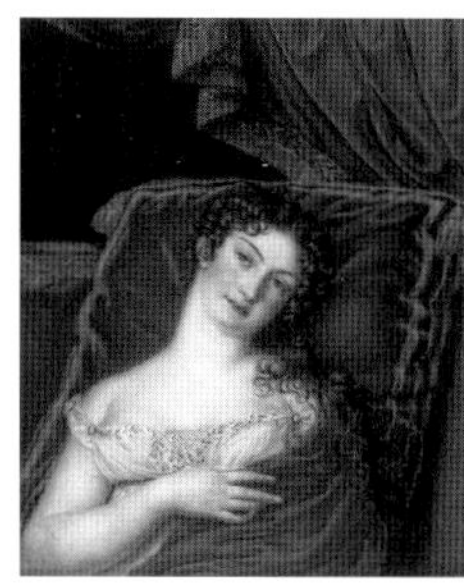

87 ADELE HOGUER

Louisa Bingham, Countess of Wemyss 1818

Enamel on porcelain, set in ormolu frame; 10.3 × 8.4cm (4 × 3⅜in); signed and dated on recto: *Adèle Hoguer / 1818*
COLLECTIONS: by family descent
REFERENCES: Schidlof 1964, II, p.819

Little is known of Adèle Hoguer, though she may be related to Blanche Lucie Hoguer (1786 – after 1839), who was born in Versailles, and was a pupil of Regnault. Blanche Hoguer exhibited miniatures painted on porcelain at the Salon in Paris in 1810, 1814, 1819, 1822, 1824 and 1827. She later exhibited her work at the Salon as Madame Thurot. Louisa Bingham, who was the fourth daughter of *Richard Bingham, 2nd Earl of Lucan* [80] and the sister of *Lady Anne Murray* [89], married Francis Wemyss Charteris Douglas, Lord Elcho, later 9th Earl of Wemyss at the British embassy in Paris in 1817.

THE EARL OF WEMYSS AND MARCH KT

88 CHRISTINA ROBERTSON

Clementina Elizabeth Drummond-Burrell, later Baroness Aveland (1809–1888) and her sister Elizabeth Susan Drummond-Burrell, later Willoughby (1810–1853) 1819

See pages 60 and 61

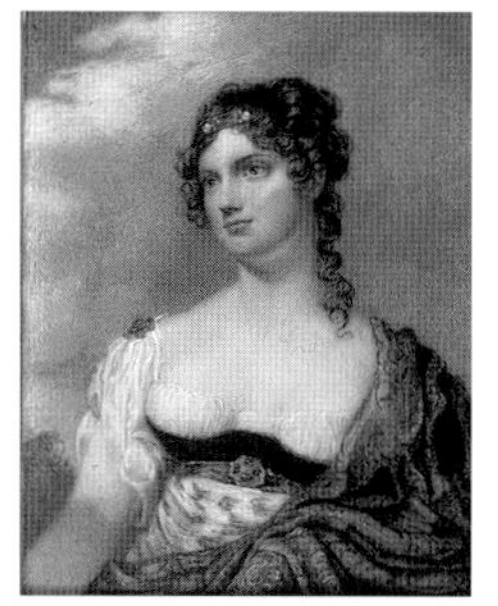

89 HENRY COLLEN AFTER GEORGE HAYTER

Lady Anne Murray (d.1850)

Watercolour on ivory, set in ormolu frame, within closing leather case; 12.3 × 10.2cm (5 × 4in); signed and dated in pen and ink on verso: *Painted by Henry Collen / from a Minia[ture] / by G Hayter – 1820 / 78 Wimpole Street*
COLLECTIONS: by family descent

Anne Bingham was the second daughter of Richard, 2nd Earl of Lucan [80] and sister of Louisa [87], who married the 9th Earl of Wemyss. In

July 1816 she married Alexander Murray MP of Broughton. Sir George Hayter (1792–1871) was a fashionable society portraitist in London. Henry Collen (1798 – after 1872) exhibited his miniatures at the Royal Academy and the Society of British Artists from 1820 to 1872.

THE EARL OF WEMYSS AND MARCH KT

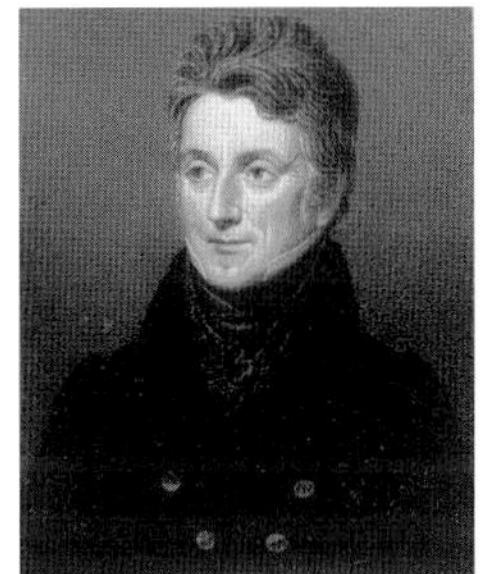

90 ATTRIBUTED TO SIR WILLIAM JOHN NEWTON

*Alexander Douglas-Hamilton, 10th Duke of Hamilton and 7th Duke of Brandon (1767–1852) c.*1815–20

Watercolour on ivory, set in gilt-slip within closing leather case; 8.8 × 6.3cm (3½ × 2½in)
COLLECTIONS: by family descent

The sitter was one of the most significant art collectors of the first half of the nineteenth century. He married Susan Beckford [92], the second daughter of Margaret Gordon, second daughter of Charles, 4th Earl of Aboyne, and of William Beckford of Fonthill Abbey in Wiltshire. Beckford was one of the wealthiest collectors of the previous generation, and the 10th Duke inherited much of Beckford's collection, which he displayed at Hamilton Palace. This miniature is close in style to the work of Sir William John Newton (1785–1869), who exhibited his portraiture at the Royal Academy and the British Institution from 1808 to 1863.

IN THE COLLECTION OF LENNOXLOVE HOUSE, HADDINGTON (BY KIND PERMISSION OF THE DUKE OF HAMILTON AND BRANDON)

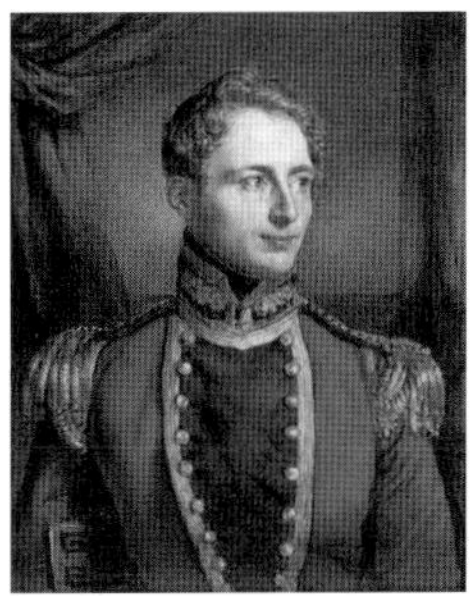

91 JOHN LINNELL

General William Moore (fl.1821 – after 1855) 1825

Watercolour on ivory, set in gilt slip within closing leather case; 11.1 × 8.9cm (4⅜ × 3½in); signed and dated on recto: *J. LINNELL f. 1825*; tooled in gold lettering on front of case: *GENERAL MOORE 1825*
COLLECTIONS: by family descent
See illustration on back cover

William Moore is shown in this miniature wearing the uniform of a colonel. He was great friend of members of the Lindsay family, and his correspondence with them survives from 1821 and 1855 (Private Collection). John Linnell (1792–1882), who as a young man befriended the elderly William Blake, painted and exhibited portrait miniatures from 1805 to 1827. He later painted oil portraits and landscapes as well as executing engravings.

PRIVATE COLLECTION

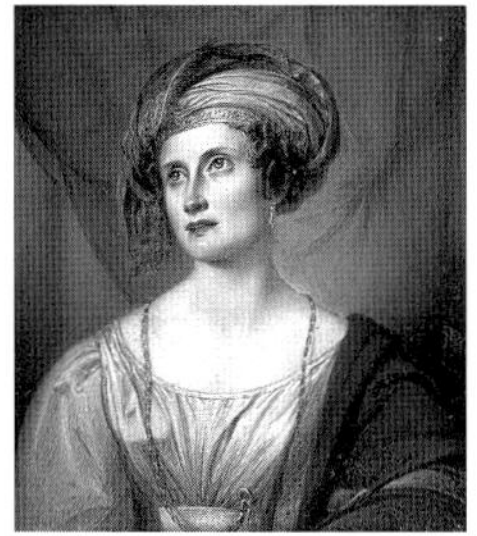

92 AUGUST GRAHL

Susan Euphemia Beckford, Duchess of Hamilton and Brandon (1786 -1859) 1827

Watercolour on ivory, set in gilt-wood frame; 14 × 11.4cm (5½ × 4½in); signed and dated on recto: *Grahl / Rome / 1827*
COLLECTIONS: by family descent
EXHIBITED: New York & London 2001–2, p.398, no.140, col. pl.

The sitter was the second daughter of Margaret Gordon, second daughter of Charles, 4th Earl of Aboyne, and of William Beckford of Fonthill Abbey in Wiltshire. Beckford was the author of *Vathek* and one of the greatest British collectors and bibliophiles of the first half of the nineteenth century. In 1810 she married Alexander Douglas-Hamilton [90], who became 10th Duke of Hamilton and 7th Duke of Brandon in 1819. August Grahl (1791–1868) was a German miniature painter, who spent much of the 1820s in Italy. This portrait was painted in Rome in 1827.

IN THE COLLECTION OF LENNOXLOVE HOUSE, HADDINGTON (BY KIND PERMISSION OF THE DUKE OF HAMILTON AND BRANDON)

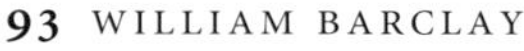

93 WILLIAM BARCLAY

Alexander William, Lord Lindsay, later 25th Earl of Crawford and 8th Earl of Balcarres (1812–1880) 1829

See pages 62 and 63

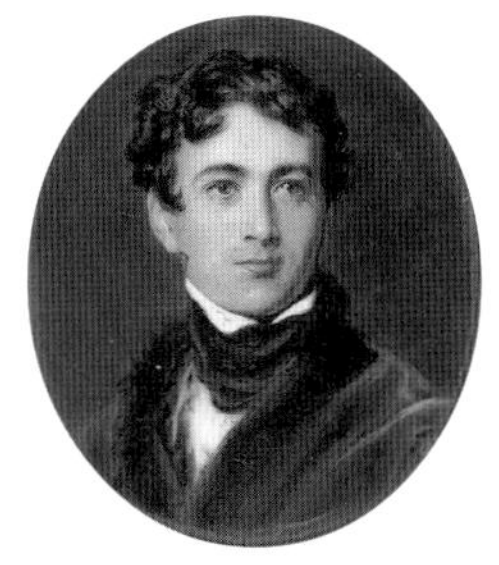

94 HENRY BONE AFTER SIR THOMAS LAWRENCE

John George Lambton, 1st Earl of Durham (1792–1840) after 1829

Enamel on copper, set in ormolu frame; 5.1cm (2in) high
COLLECTIONS: by family descent

The sitter was the father of Lady Mary Lambton, second wife of *James Bruce, 8th Earl of Elgin and 12th Earl of Kincardine* [98]. After a diplomatic career in St Petersburg, Berlin and Vienna, he was made 1st Earl of Durham in 1833 and five years later he was appointed Governor-General of the British Provinces in North America. This enamel by Henry Bone was copied after the oil by Sir Thomas Lawrence (1769–1830) now in a private collection.

THE EARL OF ELGIN AND KINCARDINE KT

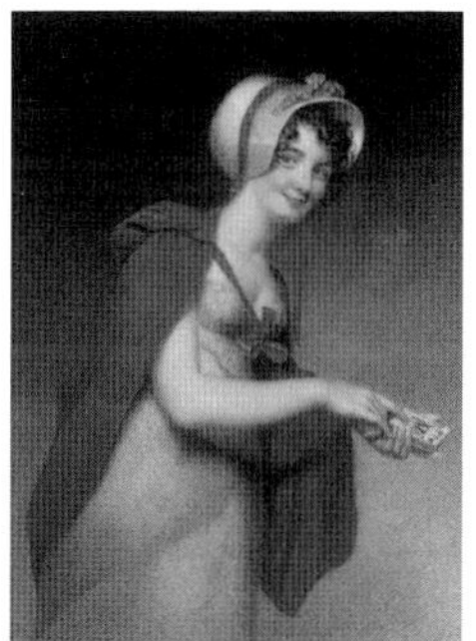

95 SAMUEL JOHN STUMP

*Mrs Honey (c.1816–1843) as a Fortune-teller c.*1830–40

Watercolour on ivory, set in gilt-metal slip within a tortoiseshell frame; 15.8 × 12.3cm (6¼ × 4½in); inscribed in pen and ink on verso: *Mrs Honey as / a 'Fortune Teller' / by 'Stump'*
COLLECTIONS: Mrs Daphne Foskett
REFERENCES: Foskett 1972, I, p.24 and opp. p.524, col. pl.XXVIII

Samuel John Stump (1778–1863), who was probably born in America, worked in London and exhibited his miniatures, watercolours and landscapes there from 1802 until 1849. Laura Honey was an actress.

PRIVATE COLLECTION

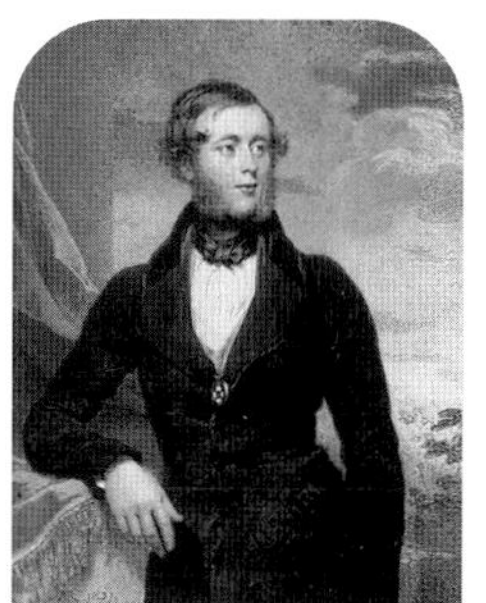

96 ANDREW ROBERTSON

James Robert, 6th Duke of Roxburghe (1816–1879) 1836–7

Watercolour on ivory, set in gilt-metal slip with arched top within a black wooden frame; 17.5 × 13.3cm (6⅞ × 5¼in); signed with monogram and dated in pencil on back of ivory: *AR 1836*
COLLECTIONS: Mrs Daphne Foskett
REFERENCES: Foskett 1972, I, p.24 and opp. p.544, col. pl.XXIX
EXHIBITED: Royal Academy, London, 1837, no.769

The sitter succeeded his father as 6th Duke of Roxburghe in 1823. He was a Lieutenant-General of the Royal Company of Archers and was made a Knight of the Thistle in 1840. He was Lord-Lieutenant of Berwickshire from 1873 until his death at Genoa. This cabinet miniature is a good example of the mature work of the Scottish artist Andrew Robertson

(1777–1845), who was one of the most fashionable miniaturists in London during the first half of the nineteenth century.

PRIVATE COLLECTION

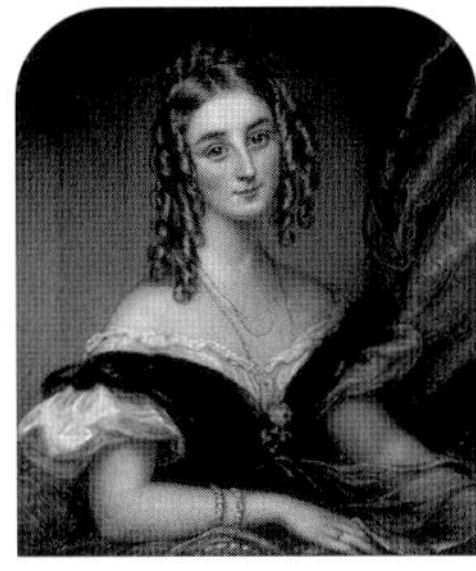

97 CHRISTINA ROBERTSON

Emily Ramsbottom, Mrs Edward Bootle-Wilbraham (d.1899) c.1840

Watercolour on ivory with arched top, set in gilt-mount, within closing case; 9.8 × 7.9cm (3⅞ × 3⅛in)
COLLECTIONS: by family descent

The sitter, who was the daughter of James Ramsbottom, married the Hon. Edward Bootle-Wilbraham, who was the second son of Edward, 1st Baron Skelmersdale, in 1841. Their fourth daughter Emily Florence married James Ludovic Lindsay, 26th Earl of Crawford and 9th Earl of Balcarres. The Scottish miniaturist, Christina Robertson (1796–1854) exhibited her miniatures in London (1823–49) and Edinburgh (1829–39), before working in St Petersburg in the later part of her career.

PRIVATE COLLECTION

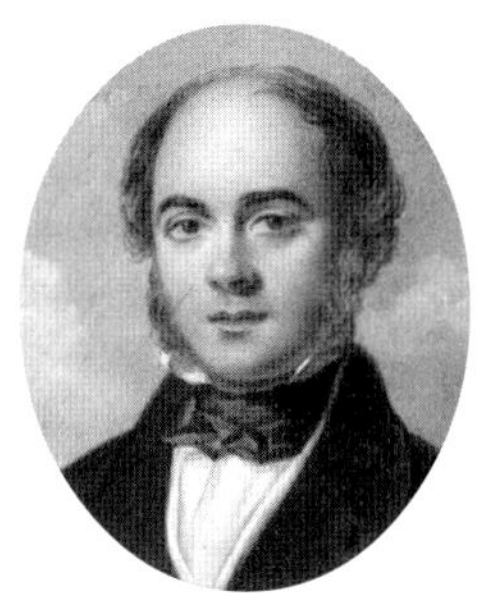

98 GEORGE RICHMOND

James Bruce, 8th Earl of Elgin and 12th Earl of Kincardine (1811–1863) c.1841

Watercolour on ivory, set in ornamental ormolu frame; 5.6 cm (2¼in) high
COLLECTIONS: by family descent
REFERENCES: Checkland 1988, opp. p.90, col. pl.8

The sitter had a distinguished career as a diplomatic pro-consul in Jamaica, Canada, India and China during a period of burgeoning British imperial power. George Richmond RA (1809–1896), who was the son of the miniaturist Thomas Richmond, began his highly successful career in London as a miniaturist, before painting portraits in oil, crayon and watercolour.

THE EARL OF ELGIN AND KINCARDINE KT

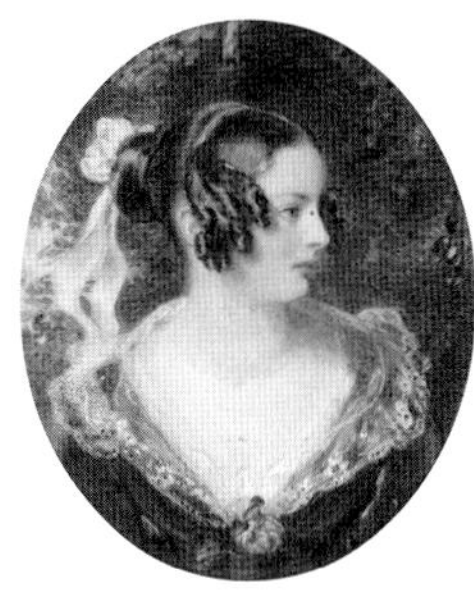

99 SIR WILLIAM CHARLES ROSS

*Elizabeth Mary Cumming Bruce, Countess of Elgin and Kincardine (1821–1843) c.*1841

Watercolour on ivory, set in ornamental ormolu frame; 8.8cm (3½in) high
COLLECTIONS: by family descent
REFERENCES: Checkland 1988, opp. p.91, col. pl.9

The sitter was the first wife of *James Bruce, 8th Earl of Elgin and 12th Earl of Kincardine* [98]. The couple, who married in 1814, had two daughters. Lady Elgin died in Jamaica, a year after her husband had taken up the post of Governor of the island. Sir William Charles Ross RA (1794/5–1860), who was of Scottish descent, was the dominant miniaturist working in London during the first part of Queen Victoria's reign.

THE EARL OF ELGIN AND KINCARDINE KT

REFERENCES

ARMSTRONG *ET AL.* 1901
Sir Walter Armstrong, J.L. Caw and R.A.M. Stevenson, *Sir Henry Raeburn*, London and New York, 1901

BARNES *ET AL.* 2004
Susan J. Barnes, Nora de Poorter, Oliver Millar, Horst Vey, *Van Dyck: A Complete Catalogue of his Paintings*, New Haven and London, 2004

BROWN 2003
Iain Gordon Brown (ed.), *Abbotsford and Sir Walter Scott: The Image and the Influence*, Edinburgh, 2003

CANNADINE 1990
David Cannadine, *The Decline and Fall of the British Aristocracy*, New Haven and London, 1990

CHECKLAND 1988
Sydney Checkland, *The Elgins, 1766–1917: A Tale of Aristocrats, Proconsuls and their Wives*, Aberdeen, 1988

COFFIN & HOFSTETTER 2000
Sarah Coffin and Bodo Hofstetter, *The Gilbert Collection: Portrait Miniatures in Enamel*, London, 2000

COOMBS 1998
Katherine Coombs, *The Portrait Miniature in England*, London, 1998

FOSKETT 1972
Daphne Foskett, *A Dictionary of British Miniature Painters*, 2 vols., London, 1972 [reprinted: Woodbridge, 1987]

FOSKETT 1979
Daphne Foskett, *Collecting Miniatures*, London, 1979

FOSTER 1926
J.L. Foster, *Dictionary of Painters of Miniatures*, London, 1926

FRASER 1878
Sir William Fraser, *The Scotts of Buccleuch*, 2 vols., Edinburgh, 1878

GIROUARD 1960
Mark Girouard, 'Drumlanrig Castle, Dumfries-shire: a seat of the Duke of Buccleuch & Queensberry', *Country Life*, CXXVII, 3 parts, nos.3312–14, 25th August and 1st and 8th September 1960, pp.378–81, 434–7 and 488–91

GREIG 1911
James Greig, *Sir Henry Raeburn,* R.A.*: his life and works, with a catalogue of his pictures*, London, 1911

INGAMELLS 1997
John Ingamells, *A Dictionary of British and Irish Travellers in Italy 1701–1800*, New Haven and London, 1997

JAMIESON 1993
Fiona Jamieson, *Drummond Castle Gardens*, [n.p.] 1993

KENNEDY 1917
H.A. Kennedy, *Early English Miniatures in the Collection of the Duke of Buccleuch* [special number of *The Studio*], London, 1917

LLOYD 2005
Stephen Lloyd, *Richard Cosway*, London, 2005

LLOYD 2005A
Stephen Lloyd, '"Elegant and graceful attitudes": the painter of the "Skating Minister"', *Burlington Magazine*, vol.CXLVII, no.1228, July 2005, pp.474–86

LOCHE & ROETHLISBERGER 1978
Renée Loche and Marcel Roethlisberger, *L'opera completa di Liotard*, Milan, 1978

LONG 1929
Basil S. Long, *British Miniaturists: 1520–1860*, London, 1929 [reprinted 1966]

MCKAY 1899
Andrew McKay, *Catalogue of the Miniatures in Montagu House belonging to the Duke of Buccleuch*, 2nd edn., London, 1899 [*The Collection of Miniatures in Montagu House*, 1st edn., 1896]

MACKENZIE-STUART 1995
A. J. Mackenzie-Stuart, *A French King at Holyrood*, Edinburgh, 1995

MAXWELL STUART 1986
Peter Maxwell Stuart, *Traquair House*, Norwich, 1986

MARSHALL 1973
Rosalind K. Marshall, *The Days of Duchess Anne: Life in the Household of the Duchess of Hamilton 1656–1716*, London, 1973 [reprinted: Edinburgh, 2000]

MILNER 1997
Catherine Milner, 'Earliest portraits by Raeburn discovered', *The Sunday Telegraph*, 23 November 1997, p.7

MURDOCH *ET AL.* 1981
John Murdoch, Jim Murrell, Patrick J. Noon and Roy Strong, *The English Miniature*, New Haven and London, 1981

MURDOCH 1992
Tessa Murdoch (ed), *Boughton House: The English Versailles*, London, 1992

MURDOCH 1997
John Murdoch, *Seventeenth-Century English Miniatures in the Collection of the Victoria & Albert Museum*, London, 1997

NICHOLAS 1973
Donald Nicholas, *The Portraits of Bonnie Prince Charlie*, Maidstone, 1973

ODNB 2004
Oxford Dictionary of National Biography, 60 vols., Oxford, 2004

SCHIDLOF 1964
Léo R. Schidlof, *The Miniature in Europe in the 16th, 17th, 18th and 19th Centuries*, 4 vols., Graz, 1964

SMAILES 1990
Helen Smailes, *The Concise Catalogue of the Scottish National Portrait Gallery*, Edinburgh, 1990

WAINWRIGHT 1989
Clive Wainwright, *The Romantic Interior: The British Collector at Home, 1750–1850*, New Haven and London, 1989

WALKER 1992
Richard Walker, *The Eighteenth and Early Nineteenth Century Miniatures in the Collection of Her Majesty The Queen*, Cambridge, 1992

WILLIAMSON 1906–8
George C. Williamson, *Catalogue of the Collection of Miniatures the Property of J. Pierpont Morgan*, 4 vols., London, 1906–8

WOOD 1917
T. Martin Wood, 'The Buccleuch Miniatures at the Victoria & Albert Museum', *The Studio: an illustrated magazine of fine & applied art*, LXIX, no.2876, January 1917, pp.163–77

ZACHS 1998
William Zachs, *The first John Murray and the late eighteenth-century London book trade*, Oxford, 1998

Exhibition Catalogues

CHANTILLY 2004
Olivier Meslay (ed.), *L'art anglais dans les collections de l'Institut de France*, Musée Condé, Chantilly, 2004

EDINBURGH 1876
Exhibition of the works of Sir Henry Raeburn, R.A., Royal Academy and National Galleries, Edinburgh, 1876

EDINBURGH 1951
Scotland Yet: Exhibition of Historic Scottish Treasures, Moubray House, Edinburgh, 1951

EDINBURGH 1965
Daphne Foskett, *British Portrait Miniatures*, The Arts Council Gallery, Edinburgh 1965

EDINBURGH 1996
Christina Robertson: A Scottish Portraitist at the Russian Court, City Art Centre, Edinburgh, 1996

EDINBURGH 1996–7
Stephen Lloyd, *Portrait Miniatures from the Collection of the Duke of Buccleuch*, Scottish National Portrait Gallery, Edinburgh, 1996–7

EDINBURGH 1999
Stephen Lloyd, *Raeburn's Rival: Archibald Skirving 1749–1819*, Scottish National Portrait Gallery, Edinburgh, 1999

EDINBURGH 2000
Aidan Weston-Lewis (ed.), *'A Poet in Paradise': Lord Lindsay and Christian Art*, National Gallery of Scotland, Edinburgh, 2000

EDINBURGH 2001
Stephen Lloyd, *Portrait Miniatures from the Clarke Collection*, Scottish National Portrait Gallery, Edinburgh, 2001

EDINBURGH 2001A
Edward Corp, *The King Over The Water: Portraits of the Stuarts in Exile*, Scottish National Portrait Gallery, Edinburgh, 2001

EDINBURGH 2003
Stephen Lloyd, *Portrait Miniatures from the Daphne Foskett Collection*, Scottish National Portrait Gallery, Edinburgh, 2003

EDINBURGH 2004
Stephen Lloyd, *Portrait Miniatures from the National Galleries of Scotland*, Scottish National Portrait Gallery, Edinburgh, 2004

EDINBURGH 2005
Stephen Lloyd, *Portrait Miniatures from the Merchiston Collection,* Scottish National Portrait Gallery, Edinburgh, 2005

EDINBURGH & LONDON 1992–3
Alastair Smart, *Allan Ramsay 1713–1784*, Scottish National Portrait Gallery, Edinburgh, and National Portrait Gallery London, 1992–3

EDINBURGH & LONDON 1995–6
Stephen Lloyd *et al.*, *Richard & Maria Cosway: Regency Artists of Taste and Fashion*, Scottish National Portrait Gallery, Edinburgh, and National Portrait Gallery, London, 1995–6

EDINBURGH & LONDON 1997–8
Raeburn: The Art of Sir Henry Raeburn 1756–1823, Royal Scottish Academy, Edinburgh, and National Portrait Gallery, London, 1997

GLASGOW 1888
International Exhibition: The Book of the Bishop's Castle, and Handbook of the Archaeological Collection, Glasgow, 1888

LONDON 1865
Samuel Redgrave (ed), *Catalogue of the Special Exhibition of Portrait Miniatures…*, South Kensington Museum, London, 1865

LONDON 1889
J. Lumsden Propert, *Exhibition of Portrait Miniatures*, Burlington Fine Arts Club, London, 1889

LONDON 1916–20
Ninety-six Miniatures from the Collection lent by the Duke of Buccleuch, H.A. Kennedy (ed.), 2nd edn., Victoria & Albert Museum, London, 1916–20 [1st edn., 1916]

LONDON 1934
Exhibition of British Art c.1000–1860, Royal Academy, London, 1934

LONDON 1960–1
The Age of Charles II, Royal Academy, London, 1960–1

LONDON 1974
Daphne Foskett, *Samuel Cooper and his Contemporaries*, National Portrait Gallery, London, 1974

LONDON 1993
Richard Walker (ed), *The Monarchy in Portrait Miniatures from Elizabeth I to Queen Victoria*, D.S. Lavender (Antiques) Ltd, London, 1993

LONDON 1996
Ian Jenkins and Kim Sloan (eds.), *Vases and Volcanoes: Sir William Hamilton and his collection*, The British Museum, London, 1996

LONDON & NEW HAVEN 2001–2
Catharine MacLeod and Julia Marciari Alexander *et al.*, *Painted Ladies: Women at the Court of Charles II*, National Portrait Gallery, London, and Yale Center for British Art, New Haven, 2001–2

NEW YORK, SAN MARINO, RICHMOND & LONDON 1996–7
Christopher Lloyd and Vanessa Remington, *Masterpieces in Little: Portrait Miniatures from the Collection of Her Majesty The Queen*, The Metropolitan Museum of Art, New York; The Huntington Library, Art Collections and Botanical Gardens, San Marino; Virginia Museum of Fine Arts, Richmond; and The Queen's Gallery, Buckingham Palace, London, 1996–7

NEW YORK & LONDON 2001–2
Derek E. Ostergard (ed.), *William Beckford, 1760–1844: An Eye for the Magnificent*, The Bard Center, New York, and Dulwich Picture Gallery, London, 2001–2

ST GERMAIN 1992
Edward Corp (ed.), *La Cour des Stuarts à Saint-Germain-en-Laye au temps de Louis XIV*, Château de Saint Germain, 1992

INDEX OF SITTERS

References are to cat.nos.